Education Policy Unravelled

Dean Garratt
Gillian Forrester

continuum

Continuum International Publishing Group

The Tower Building	80 Maiden Lane
11 York Road	Suite 704
London SE1 7NX	New York NY 10038

www.continuumbooks.com

British Library Cataloguing-in-Publication Data
A catalogue record for this book is available from the British Library.

ISBN: 978-1-4411-3073-0 (paperback)
　　　978-1-4411-6618-0 (hardcover)

Library of Congress Cataloging-in-Publication Data
Garratt, Dean.
  Education policy unravelled / Dean Garratt.
    p. cm.
Summary: "A comprehensive introduction to the nature of contemporary education policy, its purposes and political formation which supports readers to engage in contemporary policy analysis"– Provided by publisher.
  Includes bibliographical references and index.
    ISBN 978-1-4411-3073-0 (pbk.) – ISBN 978-1-4411-6618-0
  1. Education and state–Great Britain. 2. Education–Aims and objectives–Great Britain.
  I. Forrester, Gillian. II. Title.

LC93.G7K27 2012+
379.41–dc23

2011046917

Typeset by Newgen Imaging Systems Pvt Ltd, Chennai, India

Contents

Acknowledgements

To those who have helped with the thinking that has contributed to our interest and enthusiasm for this book – including anonymous referees, former colleagues and friends at work – many thanks. We would also like to thank (and apologize to) our families, without whose support and encouragement this book would not have been possible: Claire, Tom and William; Paul, Stacie and Natalie.

Introduction: The Development of Education Policy in the Modern Era

Chapter Outline

The nature of education policy

This book explores the nature of education policy, attempting to 'unravel' its meaning in the broadest and narrowest senses. The purpose of the book is to disaggregate education policy so that significant features and characteristics of policy-making and a number of related issues can be dismantled, separated out and examined indepth in order to illuminate particular and important enduring themes and trends as well as to encourage the reader to engage in deeper exploration. It is never possible to examine education policy purely on its own as a single, discrete entity. Education policy-making does not 'happen' in a vacuum or bubble, but is subject to a range of competing influences, which can be broadly categorized under the umbrella of social, political, economic, techno-logical, religious or cultural factors. The book therefore examines education policy in the context of a range of constituting factors that have all influenced and continue to impact upon education in a variety of ways. Education policy is constantly changing and, over time, different factors have had different levels of prominence; so education systems, organizations, educational activities, learners and those working in education have been shaped in a variety of ways at different points in time. Adding to this complexity is an assortment of different individuals, groups, events, movements, ideologies and perspectives that may in some way contribute to and shape policy 'problems' and 'solutions' at different historical moments. Our overriding aim in writing this book therefore rests upon conceptually 'undoing' and critically analysing the threads that together constitute the intricately woven tapestry of education and policy-making. Using concrete examples and pertinent illustrations from a variety of sources, we aim to facilitate readers' understanding of key policy issues, facilitate an appreciation of the 'contested terrain' (Ozga, 2000) of education policy research and bring life to the field of education policy.

The term 'policy' could be regarded as 'obvious' and fairly comprehensible in its own right. However, policy is an often quite loosely used term and therefore can be defined and understood in different ways. In its narrowest form policy can be considered as a statement of intent; something which is written down in a policy document, for example, and an expression of policy-makers' plans, objectives or policy descriptions of practice. In this sense, policy can be regarded as being static and fixed. Trowler (2003: 95), referring specifically to education, offers the following lucid explanation of policy as:

> a specification of principles and actions, related to educational issues, which are followed or which should be followed and which are designed to bring about desired goals.

In his conceptualization of policy Ball (1993) makes a clear distinction between policy as 'text' and policy as 'discourse'. Regarding policy as text Ball (ibid.) suggests this is concrete and exists as a written representation of policy; it is 'read'. However, Ball recognizes that while policies are officially put forward in policy documentation, it is important to comprehend that policies are unlikely to stay fixed since they are typically re-worked through speeches, media interviews, 'spin', reports, the agendas of particular individuals and so on. It is highly unlikely that policy unfolds straightforwardly from formulation to implementation and operates at the ground exactly as policy-makers originally intended. Ball (ibid.) thus acknowledges the contested, changing and negotiated character of policy, which is usually an outcome of struggles and compromises between different individuals, groups and interests involved in policy-making. A broader, more encompassing view, therefore, is not just to think of policy as a product or an outcome (such as a policy document), but rather as a *process* that is ongoing, interactional and unstable (Ozga, 2000). So, in this sense policy can be considered dynamic. Accordingly, Considine (1994: 3) provides the following definition of policy:

> In a sense everything in the policy world is really just process, the movement of people and programs around common problems such as education, transport and employment. None of these initiatives in these fields stays fixed for very long because the problems themselves keep moving and changing.

We will explore the view of policy as a process further, but first we give consideration to a common-sense concept of public policy as something constructed within the 'machinery' of the government, which we can regard as 'big-P' policy. Big-P policy comprises two key features; formal policy and informal policy. In its 'formal' sense big-P policy is sanctioned by the government and is usually legislated. In its 'informal' sense big-P policy may constitute government-approved policy initiatives that are not legislated and may reflect certain pressures from the ground level or from public expectations. One recent example of formal big-P policy is the decision in 2010 by the UK Conservative/Liberal Democrat Coalition Government to change the mechanism of funding of higher education and, essentially, transfer the cost of undergraduate tuition fees from the state to the student. This has resulted in universities being able to charge undergraduate fees of over £6,000 and up to £9,000 per year from 2012 (Sedghi and Shepherd, 2011).

Staying with the notion of big-P policy and discerning policy as a process we draw on Trowler (2003) who suggests the dynamism of policy is due to a number of sources. First, there is usually conflict of some sort between policy-makers' intentions and those who implement policy; so there will typically be differences between the rhetoric of policy and the reality of the enactment of policy on the ground. Secondly, it is important to appreciate that policy can be subject to many different interpretations, which are influenced by different standpoints and interests. In this sense, the interpretation of policy can be considered as an active process. Thirdly, the implementation of policy in practice often means the outcomes differ from policy-makers' intentions. Policy intentions, as described, are as a rule usually numerous and often of a contradictory nature. Ball (1994: 10 cited in Trowler 2003: 96) succinctly captures this form of dynamism:

> Policy is both text and action, words and deeds, it is what is enacted as well as what is intended. Policies are always incomplete insofar as they relate to or map on to the 'wild profusion' of local practice.

The example provided earlier regarding higher education demonstrates the convolution of a policy decision and its impact at ground level. Due to the devolved nature of the government in the United Kingdom what has subsequently transpired in higher education is a situation where from 2012 students who live in England will be required to pay up to the full £9,000 tuition costs in whatever UK university they attend. In contrast, students who live in Scotland can study at Scottish universities for free although if they choose to study in England they will be required to pay up to £9,000 tuition fees. Welsh students, however, will be subsidized by the Welsh Government and only required to pay tuition fees of approximately £4,000 wherever they study in the United Kingom. Students living in Northern Ireland will be required to pay approximately £4,000 if they study in Northern Ireland, but up to £9,000 elsewhere in the United Kingdom. This particular big-P policy demonstrates how the decision of a government to change funding, brought about largely as a result of a set of economic factors, will have multiple repercussions. Leaving aside the impact upon higher education institutions, the consequences for the individual student is tremendous. For some students this policy will translate to greater levels of debt. Others may consider that higher education will not be feasible and are thus deprived of higher education as a vehicle for improving one's chances and opportunities. Some may seek to study elsewhere in Europe, in countries/institutions where there are no fees, and thus become 'tuition tourists'. For example, Bawden (2011) claims that 'QR' the international career and education network has, for the first time, produced a world-ranking list of 600 universities that also compares tuition costs and further suggests that many of the top 200 global institutions have tuition fees of less than £9,000, the maximum threshold in England. Dutch institutions are presented in a favourable light as are three universities in Hong Kong, all of which offer a good range of undergraduate programmes taught in English, and at a fraction of the cost of those offered in England. There are, of course, many other attractively priced alternatives across Europe in Scandinavia, Switzerland and France, which offer competitively priced programmes for students who, in each case, are able to speak the native language. As Bawden (ibid.) explains in the case of EU institutions:

> According to the Student Loans Company, UK undergraduates wishing to study at EU universities would be eligible for a loan from that country to cover their tuition fees. If the countries also offered loans to cover living expenses, they would be able to apply for those.

Such alternatives outside the United Kingdom serve to underscore just how expensive higher education has become at home in the United Kingdom, and in England more especially. Government policies thus can have major implications for individuals, institutions and nations.

At another level, we acknowledge there are policies that are formed and enacted within localities and institutions; these could be thought of as 'little-P' policies. Little-P policies might be, for example, in a secondary school or college of further education where there is a policy on homework that has been specifically designed within and for that particular institution. This book is primarily concerned with big-P policy, however, and it is to this policy process that we now turn.

The policy process

The practice of policy-making at the national level is complicated and complex. Policy-making is not necessarily a linear or logical process, but often the reconciliation of competing ideas and interests, compromises and trade offs. Initial ideas can emerge from pieces of commissioned or non-commissioned research, different government departments, the civil service, political 'think tanks' and/or pressure groups keen to exert themselves in order to effect change. As Apple (1990) suggests in relation to the nature of competing ideologies, political tensions in policy-making are inevitable as groups with different vested interests compete for power in the struggle to make their voice heard. The formalization and formation of policy is often a convoluted process, where initially around 15 to 20 ideas are given parliamentary time in each session. From here such ideas are considered and debated, and a small number will later be selected by the Cabinet of the presiding government to become Green Papers containing big questions about policy direction and what is to be achieved.

Essentially, Green Papers are an exploratory consultative exercise, presenting a preliminary report of government proposals to stimulate public discussion and further debate around particular salient issues and themes. Often they will contain questions that the government would like the public to consider and answer, and this is where resistance is most likely to arise as different stakeholders begin to query and question aspects of the proposal under consideration. In practice, Green Papers are often commissioned by the relevant government department under circumstances in which its administration feels there is an area where new legislation is needed, or indeed where existing legislation requires some modification or amendment. Significantly, however, Green Papers make no formal commitment to action, but rather provide an opportunity for open debate and represent perhaps the first stage in the process to changing a law. Some proposals, particularly controversial ones, can take a great deal of time at this stage, before entering the report stage where Members of Parliament (MPs) are later able to introduce their thoughts and feelings (of which, more below).

Subsequently, the feedback provided from wider public consultation and research carried out by government departments in relation to the Green Paper is used to inform the production of a White Paper. White Papers are issued by the government as a statement of policy, setting out more detailed proposals for legislative change or the introduction of a new law(s). Again, there are usually opportunities for the public to comment on White Papers although such papers represent a much bolder statement of intent or precursor to a Bill, which is a draft law. In some cases, a single White Paper will transform into a Bill; in others, there may be several White Papers combined in one Bill or, alternatively, several Bills emerging from a single White Paper.

Bills are debated by MPs and members of the House of Lords and cannot usually be influenced, at this stage, by the public. Sometimes it is possible, however, to lobby individual Lords or encourage an MP to table an amendment to a Bill, or possibly influence how they might vote. The formalization of policy occurs through a series of readings after the Bill is first introduced to the House of Commons; this is the first reading. The second reading is an open debate of the Bill by Members of the House, which can sometimes be followed by a vote, although Bills introduced by the government tend to be accepted by their own MPs. The Committee Stage follows in which a cross-party committee has the role of debating, amending and agreeing to each clause of the proposed Bill before it is put to a vote in both Houses of Parliament (Commons and Lords), where its content is formally agreed and passed. A Bill does not officially become an Act (i.e. law) until it has been granted Royal Assent, which requires the Queen to agree with the Act and is usually a formality.

Ideology and discourse

The purposes of education are contested; different assumptions can be made about what education should be doing, who should be doing what and how it should be done. We deal with the aims of education elsewhere (see Chapters 2 and 6). The point we intend to make here is that education cannot be regarded as a neutral concept; it is paramount, when exploring education, to examine the relationship between policy and ideology. Ideology is a widely used term with several meanings, each of which has different implications for the process of policy formation. Historically, the term was first coined by a group of French intellectuals called 'ideologues', operating at the heart of the French Enlightenment. For them, ideology was simply an expression for the 'science of ideas', the basis for establishing authentic knowledge and truth about the social world. In the aftermath of the French revolution and following Napoleon Bonaparte's defeat at the hands of the Russian army in 1812, ideology was denounced for its 'false ideas' and so took on a more pejorative (negative) meaning. Later on, this was adopted by Marx and Engels in *German Ideology* to describe the distorted social and economic relationship between the ruling class (bourgeoisie) and the proletariat (working class), where ideology had the effect of creating an 'illusion' or type of 'false consciousness', both of which pointed to a political environment producing distortions through doctrinaire thinking. As Apple (1990) suggests, ideology 'works' precisely because its persuasive rhetoric serves to disguise the vague quality of its underlying assumptions. Such disguised assumptions render ideology legitimate since there are always aspects of the concept that remain partly hidden, with the effect that if it appears 'real' it becomes so through its consequences.

Different doctrines or 'belief systems' about what counts as knowledge are shaped politically by dominant ideas, structures and historical patterns that in turn shape social and economic behaviour. Such ideological patterns do not represent 'objective' reality 'out-there', but rather reflect the views influenced by social and historical structures. The notion that ideology produces a scenario in which a minority *dominate* while the vast majority are *dominated* is based on a conflict theory of capital and production. This takes us well beyond the argument of simple abstract theoretical distortions to directly acknowledge the effect of ideology emerging from actual capitalist practices (Freeden, 2003). In this context, it is the 'propertied' class, the class of industrial capitalists (bourgeoisie/middle class) who control the means of production, distribution and exchange and the 'property-less' or large proletariat who sell their labour for a wage, but unwittingly accept exploitation in the capitalist process. For Marx, the solution to the problem of ideology was revolution, where the proletariat would eventually identify the hidden motives of the capitalists, rise against them and thus change the social order.

In contrast with ideology's pejorative meaning it has also bequeathed a more positive one in the history of ideas. As Freeden (2003: 12–13) explains:

> while Marx condemned the social conditions under capitalism as the source of ideology illusion, Mannheim realized that it was a feature of any social environment to influence the thought processes of human beings and, moreover that knowledge was a 'co-operative process of group life'.

In this respect, ideology is not a 'falsehood' to be demystified but a manifestation of thinking or system of beliefs. Ideology thus represents a set of ideas and concepts about the social world in addition to the influence of important social and historical structures. This has resonance with the work of French social theorist Michel Foucault (1980: 118) who argued vigorously against the concept of ideology conceived as 'false consciousness': 'the notion of ideology appears to me to be difficult to make use of . . . like it or not, it always stands in virtual opposition to something else which is supposed to count as truth'. Indeed for Foucault, like Mannheim, there is no escaping the influence of different systems of ideas that can be only properly understood through historical analysis. In Foucault's (ibid.: 131) idiom, ideology is 'truth' not a 'falsehood' or mere pernicious myth. It is:

> a thing of the world: it is produced only by virtue of multiple forms of constraint. And it induces regular effects of power. Each society has its regime of truth, its 'general politics' of truth – that is, the types of discourse it accepts and makes function as true; the mechanisms and instances that enable one to distinguish true and false statements; the means by which each is sanctioned; the techniques and procedures accorded value in the acquisition of truth; the status of those who are charged with saying what counts as true.

Education policy is therefore influenced by different ideologies (political and educational), values, attitudes and beliefs. The 1945–79 era was fuelled by a social democratic/one-nation, conservative perspective whereby there was largely a political consensus about the purpose of education in reducing social inequalities, improving social mobility and creating a more meritocratic society. State intervention was deemed necessary to support educational provision and facilitate equality of opportunity. There was, however, a change in emphasis in the 1980s and 1990s and a shift away from the social democratic consensus towards the market as the main source of resource distribution. Many initiatives were introduced to establish the conditions for a competitive market as part of the wider New Right agenda of change across the public sector. The political New Right represents a coalition of neo-liberal and neo-conservative thinking. The former promotes the virtue of a free-market economy as a more effective mechanism for the distribution of social resources, competition, privatization and individual liberty, while the latter privileges tradition, hierarchy, authority and social order. Neo-conservatism is committed to the regeneration of traditional moral values, authority, the virtues of a strong state and intervention by the government to achieve these. Under neo-conservatism individual liberty remains important but ultimately defers to the authority of established government and the concept of 'nation' (Scruton, 1980). Paradoxically, these strands came together under the New Right ideology. Educational ideologies also inform and influence teaching and learning and comprise traditionalism (transmission of heritage, subject-centred) progressivism (child-centredness) and enterprise (emphasis on core skills, the workplace) (Trowler, 2003). Political ideologies can crudely be married up with educational ideologies as follows: social democracy – progressive; neo-conservatism – traditionalism; and neo-liberalism – enterprise. All of these ideological forces are competing, have different emphases at different times and work towards different goals.

The New Labour Government (1997–2010) pledged to move beyond ideological boundaries espousing a 'what works' agenda based on research evidence and went to some lengths to present policies as distinct from previous administrations through the discourse (rhetorical device) of modernization. Discourse, by definition, is concerned with communication and refers to talk, conversation and dissertation. In the social sciences its meaning is extended to incorporate statements, knowledge and ideas (Jupp, 1996) that are dominant at a particular time, place and amid certain sets of people (in this case policymakers) and which are held in relation to other groups of people (e.g. teachers). Such statements, knowledge and ideas provide authoritative explanations of what is problematic and why and the proposed course of action. However, and as Jupp (1996) maintains, the provision of some explanations inevitably excludes other alternatives and so the application of power is implicit in the use of such knowledge.

Discourse and discourse analysis are often associated with the work of Michel Foucault. According to Foucault discourse or discursive practices determine how certain acts become accepted or self-evident (taken as known) at particular times and how these become established as being 'natural'. Legge's (1995: 326, 2) definition of the concept of discourse is both succinct and explanatory and so is quoted here in full:

'Discourse' refers to the way in which things are discussed and the argumentation and rhetoric used to support what is said. It also refers to 'reading between the lines' – what remains unspoken or taken-for granted, such as assumptions or evasions. Crucially, discourse analysis deals with issues of representation. That is, it starts with the premise that words do not merely reflect what is being talked about, but they actually construct and even constitute what is being talked about.

What Legge (ibid.) is claiming here is the way people talk and think about the world reflects the dominance of particular discourses. Ball (1990: 18) puts this another way asserting, 'discourses construct certain possibilities for thought . . . We do not speak the discourse. The discourse speaks us'. Discourses are more than just words or language, but constitute a way of acting in the social world as well as describing it. What is thought and what can be said is not some objective truth about that world, though these ways of thinking and talking tend to become invisible because they are simply accepted as the truth. In this way people's thought processes can themselves come to embody and make stronger particular regimes of power and coercion. The discourses of the more powerful groups in society are more likely to be influential and gain legitimacy, often gaining support in the form of legislation, while the perspectives of subordinate groups are marginalized. In this way the dominance of certain discourses affects how an issue is understood and also helps to establish certain boundaries on the possibilities and limits of debate, how individuals should act and, in some instances, how the state should intervene. Some discourses are thus more influential than others or considered more legitimate and natural. Ball (1993) refers to 'policy as discourse' and Levitas (1998: 3) discusses the 'language of politics as a discourse'. These ideas are drawn upon in this book for making sense of the tensions around 'official' discourses.

Policy developments in the modern era: An historical overview

It is a fact of the modern era that rarely a week goes by without an educa-tion-related 'story' being reported in the media or an education-related initiative mooted or officially announced by policy-makers.

Policy-makers, commentators, educational 'experts', educational practitioners and professionals, students and pupils, along with the everyday
person in the street typically contribute to educational debates, which are
frequently given high profile by the media. As such, it is difficult to imagine
earlier times when education was not so prominent and not even thought
of as particularly newsworthy; education has became a growing political
issue since the mid-1970s. In order to comprehend education policy and
policy-making in the present, modern day however it is imperative to look
back and examine the position education has held in the past, to view
changes in education policy and educational provision over time from a
historical perspective and to consider the political ideologies, educational
ideologies and the discourses at play. This approach provides an explanatory framework for the book as it emphasizes key themes underpinned by
the social, political and economic context. Key moments that are especially
significant in education policy are outlined below, although more details
surrounding some of these particular 'landmarks' are found in the subsequent chapters.

The landmark legislation of the Elementary Education Act of 1870
(also known as the Forster Act), a highly significant 'event' in the history
of education, essentially signalled the beginning of the present state-
maintained system of education in England. The introduction ten years
later of compulsory school attendance was followed in 1891 by legislation
that led to the provision of most elementary education free of charge.
These pieces of legislation marked a change in perspectives about
education moving it from being a purely private concern of families or
individuals towards being the public concern of the state. Indeed, many
held the view that the principle of 'universality' in the provision of
education for the masses would be a dangerous undertaking; an educated
population would potentially upset the existing status quo of social stratification (Chitty, 2009). Elementary education was deliberately kept at a
low level and comprised a basic 3R's curriculum, transmitted via didactic
methods. In many ways this rudimentary education encouraged the
docility, obedience and passivity of pupils and also their teachers.
Initiative was discouraged so as not to 'overeducate' the working classes
whereby they could learn to improve beyond their station in life. The
Revised Code (see Chapter 4) represented the state's attempt to exert
some control over education for the lower classes of the population

and also have some bearing on generating social consensus at a time of industrialization, social upheaval and change. While there was a building programme and Board schools were constructed, the nature of elementary education in providing a basic level of education for working class children remained relatively unchanged until 1944.

The post-war era of optimism, reconstruction and potential economic growth led to a more interventionist approach by the state in most areas of social life and it was perceived that education could address society's inequalities and problems. A political consensus about the purpose of education in a social democracy ensued with the social-democratic ideology of 'equality of opportunity' as its driving force. Thus it was deemed that every child should have educational opportunities regardless of background and there was a massive investment in education in the post-war years. The Education Act of 1944 (also known as the Butler Act) is highly significant legislation as it established a unified system of free, compulsory schooling for children aged 5 to 15. Free secondary educational provision for all resulted in the division of grammar, secondary modern and technical schools. This was not specified in the act, but became known as the tripartite system. Due to the lack of technical schools however, the reality was a bipartite system. Children were allocated to one of these schools according to their ability, which was ascertained through the 11 plus examination. Only some years later was it evident that the success or failure of children at 11 years and their attendance in grammar, technical or secondary modern schools was effectively reinforcing social class differences and reproducing the existing social order.

By the 1960s the Labour Government was moving towards a system of comprehensive education. The emerging progressive curriculum and methods transformed primary education and pedagogy from its previous traditional emphasis towards a more child-centred approach. From 1944 to the mid-1970s teachers enjoyed relative autonomy and effective control over curricula, content and pedagogic methods. They drew on public and political support, as knowledgeable, trustworthy professionals and worked in partnership with Local Education Authorities (LEAs) and the Ministry of Education (later Department for Education and Science (DES)). By the late 1960s economic conditions were changing in Britain as a consequence of dwindling world economies. This inevitably impacted upon funding for education, which was increasingly regarded as expensive, while there was mounting public concern over education and educational standards. However, regardless of the evidence for these assertions (Pring, 1992), the economic crises of the 1970s, along with increasing levels of unemployment, fuelled discontent; education was not delivering its promises. The mid- to late 1970s were marked by mounting anxiety, public and political concern over standards resulting in demands for educational reform and greater accountability of schools and teachers.

The 'Black Papers' (Cox and Dyson, 1969a; 1969b; 1970; Cox and Boyson, 1975; 1977) were a series of publications by right-wing academics and policy groups which condemned child-centred, progressive education and advocated a return to traditional teaching methods and disciplines. What became known as the 'William Tyndale Affair' (involving a Junior School in Islington, London, which utilized radical progressive methods against the wishes of parents) added to the perceived 'crisis' in education and resulted in sensational media headlines. This was the beginning of the scrutiny of education by the media, which we are so familiar with today. In 1976, the 'Great Debate' in education came about following an unprecedented speech by Prime Minister James Callaghan. His speech at Ruskin College, Oxford, focused on public concerns about falling standards, pupil dissatisfaction, the economic relevance of education and its social failure; it brought education into the spotlight as an area for public debate. The speech is highly significant as it set the agenda for education policy that would ensue in the following years. Critics of education were concerned about the influence of child-centred approaches, progressive teaching methods and the monopoly of teachers over curricula content and pedagogy. From the mid-1970s it was deemed that school leavers had inadequate skills and knowledge for the workplace. Throughout the 1980s the blame for the decline in British industry and commerce and the high levels of unemployed youth rested with ineffective teachers. There were calls for the DES to have greater involvement in the shaping of the curriculum, and more control over the LEAs and teachers. Essentially, there was a call for a more disciplined structure of learning at all stages in the system, a 'core curriculum' of basic knowledge, more vocational training and there was mounting pressure for accountability. Education became more instrumentally focused from the mid-1970s along with a discourse relating to the view that the role of schools was to prepare pupils for the workplace.

The 1988 Education Reform Act (ERA) is another landmark piece of legislation; it brought a tidal wave of reforms the effects of which were unprecedented and far reaching. The ERA empowered the Secretary of State for Education to prescribe a National Curriculum for state-maintained schools, creating greater central control over educational content and dramatically changing teachers' ways of working. A mandatory national system of pupil assessment, in the form of Standard Assessment Tasks (SATs) was established; SATs were located in four discrete Key Stages for children aged 5 to 16. Children were assessed against the expected 'standard' for their age to ascertain their level of achievement. The introduction of league tables encouraged schools to compete by exposure to market forces and performance indicators and provided comparative information for parents. It also ensured accountability. This period of time saw huge swathes of directives from the government to schools (Webb and Vulliamy, 1996) along with rafts of 'non-statutory' advice from the National Curriculum Council (NCC) and the School Examinations and Assessment Council (SEAC). Up until this point there had largely been a reluctance by policy-makers to determine methods or the 'how' of teaching in schools. Increasingly, however, the Secretary of State for Education intervened both in curricula content and pedagogy. Teachers' work intensified and resulted for stress and burnout in some because of the pressure to implement directives and maximize pupil outcomes.

In 1992, the Office for Standards in Education (OfSTED) was established to monitor activities in schools and ensure the 'proper' delivery of the curriculum. This level of external surveillance was to ascertain that schools were complying with the government's agenda. 'Failing schools', those falling short of the required standards and located towards the bottom of league tables, were thus readily identifiable and led to the 'naming and shaming' of schools. Through Local Management of Schools (LMS) schools were empowered to manage their own budget, set their own expenditure, appoint, promote and dismiss their own staff as required and assume responsibility for the marketing of their school. The market model of schooling also demanded different types of schools so that 'consumers of education', that is parents, had more choice. In accordance to this, City Technology Colleges and Grant-maintained Schools were established through the ERA providing diversity in the system while reintroducing a system of selective education. Conservative policies for education between 1979 and 1997 ensured greater centralization and control. When the New Labour Government took up office in 1997 the expectation was the incoming government would be different. What transpired, however, over the next 11 years, was essentially tighter governmental control.

New Labour explicitly stated that education would be its number one priority. New Labour's early educational reforms largely consolidated those of the previous Conservative administration; there were few policy reversals. The most notable difference was the reluctance by New Labour to rely merely on market forces to raise standards in schools, but to intervene more directly in education (Ball, 2008). Centralization increased through the setting of national targets and government intervention was proclaimed necessary in order to ensure the government's ultimate aspirations of 'raising standards' in schools were met. Education was given greater prominence for economical purposes, teachers once again found themselves under attack from policy-makers and there was public criticism (Phillips and Furlong, 2001). 'Modernization' was the mantra of the New Labour, but at the same time the prescriptive pedagogies, especially in primary schools, detailed content and methods for the daily teaching of literacy and numeracy. This level of intervention and prescription was, arguably, far from modern and resonating with the Elementary School Code of the late nineteenth century system. Teaching materials were devised for teachers such that they 'delivered' the curriculum. A revised programme for trainee teachers focused on the standards and strategies. The top-down, standards agenda with intervention and prescription was enforced by OfSTED.

Fairclough (2000) is just one commentator who has critiqued the language and rhetoric of the former New Labour in order to analyse and understand the practices of the party's approach to government and politics. The analysis of language is particularly important in New Labour's political approach because of its 'promotional way of governing' and 'the management of perception through "media spin" – constant monitoring and manipulating how issues are presented in the media' (ibid.: 157).

Fairclough (ibid.) made a distinction between three different aspects of political language namely; style, discourse and genre, though he notes that these operate concurrently. From his detailed examination of an assortment of texts, including political speeches and official documents, he argues that the logic of New Labour was constructed in its political discourse. He maintains:

> Texts are processes in which political work is done – work on elaborating political discourses, as well as the rhetorical work of mobilising people behind political discourses . . . text analysis adds to . . . discourse analysis . . . it shows how the work of politics or government is partly done in the material of texts – it gets into the texture of texts, so the political and governmental processes which are going on there can be unpicked. Without text analysis we simply miss the important aspect of political and governmental work.
> (Fairclough, 2000: 158)

Fairclough (ibid.) suggests New Labour successfully positioned itself through the construction of a new political discourse, which incorporated elements of both old left and new right politics and positioned its ideological thinking as 'the Third Way'. Le Grand (1998: 27), in a discussion of the Third Way, suggests there was a commitment to 'robust pragmatism' and the idea that 'what's best is what works'. He argues that New Labour appeared to take a broad-minded or eclectic approach in policymaking rather than the set of neo-liberal ideas that essentially underpinned the approach to reform of the preceding Conservative administration. According to Flynn (1999: 586) this included 'elements from neo-liberalism, communitarianism, and social democracy' or for Gewirtz (2002: 166) it was a 'contradictory and complex mix of neo-liberal, authoritarianism and humanistic policies for social justice'. For Hodgson and Spours (1999: 8) New Labour's Third Way was positioned between European values of social democracy, social justice and inclusion and the employment-orientated, flexible labour markets of the United States. However, whatever the ideological or political origins, there existed a resolve for New Labour to contemplate 'the use of techniques tried elsewhere' (Cabinet Office, 1999: 38) and adopt them in practice if they were considered feasible, were likely to produce the desired outcomes and meet the government's goals of modernization.

Fairclough (2000) asserts that the political discourse of New Labour was not stable but in a state of constant flux and adaptation because of the condition of shifting relations within the political environment at home and abroad and also other environments, for example, the world of business. Fairclough (ibid.) maintains the New Labour Government articulated its policies in a particularly shrewd manner in order to control public perception. Jones (1999), taking a similar line, exposes what he regarded as the 'manipulation' of the news agenda by New Labour, the 'hyping up [of] government initiatives' and 'engineering the right "build-up" to a big political announcement' (Jones, 1999: 71). This he argues was evident by the doubling in number of special advisers (from 38 to 73) whose prime function he noted, quoting the Guardian journalist Hugo Young, was 'explaining what the minister wants to get across: the guardians of access and the messengers of perception' (Jones, 1999: 73). New Labour, he maintains, placed a great amount of energy into ensuring the presentation of policy was executed 'positively and attractively' (Jones, 1999: 102). The reading of policy documents in this era of policymaking and onwards needs, therefore, to be assessed against the political backdrop of the time and also bearing in mind the trappings of 'media spin'.

The policies of the Conservative/Liberal Democrat Coalition Government from May 2010 onwards have signalled further change in education policy though, arguably, there is a different emphasis rather than any clear policy distinction. The policies emerging from the Department for Education (DfE), which immediately replaced New Labour's Department for Children Schools and Families, exhibit similar policy tensions to those that existed under the Thatcher and Major Conservative Governments between 1979 and 1997. Once again, the materializing policies have a neo-liberal emphasis of diversity and choice, primacy of markets and a minimal role for the state. Parents (and students in higher education) remain conceptualized as 'consumers' in an education marketplace with a mantra of greater choice. Such examples can be found in the extension of the schools' academies programme, via the Academies Act 2010, which has enabled outstanding schools to apply for academy status, with the programme also extended to the primary sector. This purportedly creates more diversity of provision, although this is a contested area of policy (Gunter, 2010). New types of school, 'Free Schools', have enabled parents, other groups and private providers to establish and run their own schools; again greater choice and diversity is advocated. This policy direction emanates from a Swedish model (see Chapter 7), but which essentially creates greater fragmentation in the education system (Wigborg, 2010). The *laissez-faire* ('leave to do') liberalism of Coalition Government (primarily Conservative party) policy-making is, however, inextricably coupled with Conservative beliefs in traditional curricula 'subjects' and methods of instruction, discipline and authority, and a strong state that has in place mechanisms of surveillance and accountability measures to ensure compliance with government policy. Michael Gove, the Secretary of State for Education, is keen to restore traditional subjects into schools' curricula, along with traditional teaching methods. Also, in order to improve the quality of teachers, a more rigorous application process for teacher training has been introduced, notably changes afoot to the Post Graduate Certificate of Education (PGCE), an expansion of Teach First, aimed at getting the highest performing graduates into teaching, and Teach Now, originally mooted as a 'troops of teachers' programme, that targets army professionals and those in other high-flying careers who would bring to the teaching role, according to Gove (2009), training, discipline, leadership and inspiration. Other indications of continuity and change revolve around: Reforms of the National Curriculum, league tables, the exam system, the standards agenda, inspection (targeting of failure) and teachers' pay and conditions; schools having more freedom to make local decisions; greater powers to schools to address bullying and enforce discipline; and the payment to schools of a pupil premium for those in deprived areas. Overall however, the 'what works agenda' based on 'evidence', which purportedly informed much of New Labour's policy-making, has seemingly shifted more towards 'gut instinct', 'non-academic and even anecdotal evidence' which is 'very limited and selective' in nature (Exley and Ball, 2011: 105).

As has been illustrated above, education encapsulates a range of different competing traditions, ideologies and educational philosophies that have permeated its culture at different historical moments and continue to do so. These may be viewed as complementary or contradictory or a mixture of both. Nevertheless, we have the vantage point of being able to look back and explore the legacies and recurring themes in education.

Purpose and structure of the book

Each subsequent chapter attempts to disentangle particular strands of a broad set of substantive issues as they relate to a variety of education policy areas. We take a critical perspective of policy-making and our analysis is situated within the context of broader social, political and economic movements such as neo-liberalism and globalization. The structure of the book is as follows.

Chapter 2 begins with a provocative question of whether education leads to improvement or social control. It then moves to examine the aims of education in order to question what our society should be like, and asks what 'good citizenship' might entail. Following this we present a critical analysis of successive policies for citizenship education in the secondary curriculum in England. We focus here specifically on the absence of 'race' and ethnic politics in order to show how citizenship education is formulated in ways that often constrain (as well as enhance) the possibilities for social improvement in and through education, and across the life course. Finally, we review the change in emphasis in policy from New Labour to the Conservative/Liberal Democrat Coalition Government, and consider how such planned policies and discourses around citizenship and inclusion, participation and community have started to evolve since the last general election, with implications for the reconfiguration of education in terms of improvement, regulation and control.

Chapter 3 examines education policies in Britain in relation to social justice giving emphasis to the tensions manifested in the education policies of previous and current governments. The chapter considers three discernable philosophical traditions in its analysis namely, liberal-humanist, market-individualistic and social-democratic. We show how policies promoted as providing greater equality of opportunity and access do not necessarily lead to equitable educational outcomes. The evolving primary curriculum is the focus of Chapter 4 and we provide a genealogical analysis illustrating how it has changed over time. In doing so we demonstrate how the curriculum has been a site of conflict whereby, historically, education policy has enabled the shifting of control over curricula content and pedagogy as policy-makers have attempted to address a range of contemporary social, economic and political issues. In doing so the chapter explores the 'colonization' of the primary curriculum and the de-professionalization of teachers.

In Chapter 5 we examine the relationship and tensions between the process of education and modern economy. We examine how the notion of what counts as relevant and real in educational terms has tended to become conflated with the changing preferences of modern politicians, while simultaneously evolving alongside more radical, structural change in the political economy within a regime of neo-liberalism. Initially taking an historical perspective, we reflect upon the birth of instrumentalism, in particular the academic and vocational divide, the resonance of which has created a legacy for the process of policy formation today. We analyse in some detail the formation and development of policy in the modern era, since the Great Debate up to the present, charting important continuities and nuances along the way. Finally, we question whether post-compulsory education may have failed in two senses, both as a means to address the economic imperative and as a panacea to virtuous social policy.

The 'economics of education' is the theme of Chapter 6 in which we critically examine the increasing role of market solutions in public sector policy. In particular, we focus upon the intrusion of economics in state education, which has produced not only a radical reconfiguration of education policy but a more recent alignment of education with human capital theory. Against this backdrop, we present a set of genealogies of policy discourse in higher education, tracing the various moves, continuities and changes in policy-making, where, over the last 15 years, widespread systemic and institutional change has taken place. We analyse how neo-liberal policy imperatives in higher education have led to a radical marketization of the sector and an equally radical emphasis on commercial activity, the commodification of knowledge and creation of so-called university products. This, we suggest, has served to produce divisions between the more and less well-off, and created an inequitable system in which the virtue of welfare-capitalism has been seriously compromised.

In Chapter 7 we examine the nature and meaning of globalization and its impact on education systems. An international, comparative stance is adopted to show that, in spite of the influence of globalization, significant differences remain in the construction of policy between different education systems. The chapter identifies key differences in the overlapping discourses of globalization, policy-learning and policy-borrowing. Particular cases are drawn upon to illuminate instances of policy convergence and divergence and these highlight the tensions and points of resistance that impede the transfer of policy from one context to another.

Finally, in Chapter 8 we reflect upon what it means to unravel policy before presenting a 'futures perspective' on education in which we consider a number of possibilities and contrasting visions. In this we attempt to displace the discourse of neo-liberalism with an alternative philosophy and language for educational change and social justice. Using a variety of radical examples that might usefully inform the development of future policy-making, we invite the reader's critical involvement in policy analysis to create more challenging intellectual conditions and hopefully further realize a more socially just and democratic future.

Education: Improvement or Control?

Chapter Outline

Introduction

The title of this chapter, which implies a choice between two contrasting and often conflicting educational outcomes, is a bit misleading. The idea that such concepts of improvement and control are essentially incompatible ignores the possibility of a system in which instrumental aims are actively encouraged. Viewed differently, for example, education for social control can be more directly aligned with a pragmatic notion of social and educational improvement, where better regulation and 'control' implies the prospect of a system of enhanced possibilities for social engineering. Such a system existed, for example, in Victorian Britain, where a key aim in the establishment of compulsory elementary education post 1870, and the emergence of secondary education at the turn of the twentieth century, was to address growing concerns about the rise and role of the 'raggedy' working classes

(David, 1980). A similar case can be made from an economic perspective, in which education more explicitly supports the needs of business and industry in a capitalist system, a system which, in turn, serves to reinforce a division of labour (and hence control) along class-based lines (see Chapter 5). However, our purpose here in contrasting the outcomes of 'improvement' and 'control' as binary opposites is merely to draw attention to the philosophical aims of education in such a way that their social and moral purpose can amount to more than a functionalist view. Thus, in the broadest sense, we appeal to the idea that education might actually produce an intelligent participatory democracy, in which young people are capable of thinking autonomously and, with this, developing the required forms of knowledge, skills and attitudinal dispositions that allow them to fulfil their individual potential, however so conceived.

The question of what shape or form education should take in order to address such concerns regarding the importance of autonomy and participation in learning is something that all citizens are entitled to deliberate. As White (1982: 1) notes, such difficult questions relating to the wider aims and purposes of education are aligned with broader conceptual, social and political questions like: 'what should our society be like?' From this, a variety of perspectives are produced, giving rise to different value positions and often contested ideological visions of the future (Ranson, 1994). Such diversity across a spectrum of national and institutional boundaries and cultural affiliations creates a platform for the constitution and further definition of educational aims, conceived largely as an active and mutually reciprocal process. In this sense, the concept of participation is somewhat akin to Crick's (2000) reading of the Ancients in which the aims of education and presuppositions of citizenship rest firmly upon a 'sharing of social power among the citizens of the same [] land: this is what they called liberty' (Crick, 2000: 147). From this, we can usefully extrapolate that 'good education', and hence education for 'improvement' is expressly related to 'good citizenship', which in turn relies upon a notion of autonomy and participation, as well as equity and social justice (see Chapter 3) to ensure that all citizens are treated with equal dignity and respect.

Pause and ponder

Think about the different aims and purposes of education, including the following educational models: liberal democracy, social replication of labour, cultural socialization and cultural transformation and vocationalism.

(1) What is your personal philosophy of education?

(2) What are the advantages and disadvantages of implementing your philosophy in mainstream education?

(3) Which groups within society would benefit most from this approach to education?

Against this political backdrop, we present a critique of citizenship education in England as a means to illustrate the contested terrain of educational aims and purposes through successive policies for citizenship in the secondary curriculum. Throughout, we question the extent to which such policies provide a reputable means for social and educational improvement, or whether, alternatively, they operate more coercively as a form of planned regulation and social control. In this, the analysis concentrates specifically on the absence of 'race' and ethnic politics[1] in order to show how successive policies for citizenship education have been formulated in ways that often constrain (as well as enhance) the possibilities for social improvement in and through education and across the life course. Finally, we review the change in emphasis in policy from New Labour to the Conservative/Liberal Democrat Coalition Government, and consider how such planned policies and discourses (the concept of discourse is explained more fully in Chapter 1) around citizenship and inclusion, participation and community have started to evolve since the last general election with implications for the reconfiguration of education in terms of improvement, regulation and control.

A beginning: *Education for citizenship*

In providing an historical overview of policy for citizenship education spanning the last two decades, the chapter begins by focusing on three significant documents: *Education for citizenship* (NCC, 1990), *Education for citizenship and the teaching of democracy in schools* (QCA, 1998) and the *Curriculum review: Diversity and citizenship* (DfES, 2007). In a sense, it could be argued that such a selection is not strictly comparable, since the first two documents (NCC, 1990; QCA, 1998) were clearly influenced by the Speaker's Commission on Citizenship (1990) – an eclectic assemblage of educationalists, industrialists, two bishops and a politician from each of the three main political parties – which gave considerable political weight to their discursive formation. Moreover, *Education for citizenship* emerged under a Conservative Government (1979–97) whose political rationality was to make education more efficient and standardized, and thereby erase all notions of ideology and politics from curriculum policy and discourse (Pykett, 2007).

Later, the Speaker's Commission had political resonance in the discourse of the New Labour policy, where *Encouraging citizenship* became part of a 'social panacea': a discursive landscape of social and educational reform in which the behaviour 'of the whole child as citizen' came under increasing regulation and surveillance (Pykett, 2007: 304). In contrast, *Diversity and citizenship* (DfES, 2007), commissioned by the Department for Education and Skills, was a low key affair, developed in-house and without cross-party political representation. It emerged from a wave of 'inter-ethnic group violence' (Kiwan, 2008: 18), 'fears about "home grown terrorism"' (Osler, 2009: 86), policy developments around community cohesion (Home Office, 2001a; 2001b; 2002) and, later, the Nationality, Immigration and Asylum Act (TSO, 2002), thus prompting changes in the process of naturalization (Home Office, 2005; Kiwan, 2008). However, the apparent incommensurability of the selected documents does not negate the fact that the politics of 'race' is consistently present even in its absence in the policy discourse of citizenship education. Put simply, it is conspicuous by its absence. Moreover, all three documents act as crucial signifiers of (and critical moments in) recent curriculum developments and the teaching of citizenship in schools: first through non-statutory guidance (NCC, 1990), then statutory provision (QCA, 1999) and, finally, in providing a fourth strand to citizenship education in England (DfES, 2007).

Against this political backdrop, the analysis draws upon the historical antecedents of the politics of 'race' and white supremacy in Britain.

It examines the relationship between notions of equality and 'difference' and usefully considers how the process of policy formation to 'include' and 'omit' or, indeed, 'select-in' and 'select-out' particular discourses around citizenship serves both to enable and/or constrain (Giddens, 1987) notions of equity and social justice. This is especially significant given that schools are regarded as important repositories of social and moral values, where teachers have a duty to raise the level of political literacy among young people, not least as part of the formal requirement of the revised curriculum for citizenship education (in England) (DfES, 2007) but more especially for moving into the context of the Coalition Government with emergent notions of the 'Big Society' (of which, more later).

However, we begin by addressing the document *Education for citizenship* (NCC, 1990), which provides an initial reference point for the absent presence of race within a 'neutral' and de-politicized policy discourse. The articulation of rights and responsibilities presumes a liberal understanding that all individuals *qua* citizens are equal and all communities are unimpeded by structural inequalities. Society is fair and just under the rule of law that operates to ensure no infringements occur and that equality exists between 'different types of community' within a 'pluralist society' (NCC, 1990: 6). The liberal conception thus assumes a fundamental equality of rights and responsibilities, as a means to counteract the negative consequences of a market-driven economy (Miller, 2000). As such, on the face of things, it may be assumed that such policy promotes a form of education for social 'improvement'.

However, the absence of a discourse on social rights and the welfare state provides further evidence of the politicized nature of the document presented as a largely neutral and de-politicized formation, thereby obscuring the 'politically informed criteria and standards' that the authors' 'own use of the concept [of citizenship] unavoidably incorporates' (Carr, 1991: 374). This suggests two things discursively in terms of citizenship education policy. First, the lack of any serious consideration of social rights means that structural inequalities and social injustice around 'race' is casually overlooked, since, despite appearances, 'neutrality is an impossible goal' (Kymlicka, 1995: 108) in any liberal model of citizenship. Secondly, this important omission (and tacit condonation) suggests that the relationship between the citizen and state is conceived in terms that are explicitly contractual (Miller, 2000). This parallels with the politics of the New Right and libertarian conception of citizenship where the dominant discourse translates to a 'naturalized' politics of citizenship education, combining an uncritical and depoliticized knowledge of how the institutions of government work with a passive socialization into the status quo (Carr, 1991). Indeed, this is hardly surprising given the political context of a Conservative administration under which the document emerged, and whose principal purpose was to achieve a muted consideration, if not complete and permanent erasure of more radical forms of social and political engagement. Such statements have greater resonance in the context of their social and political emergence.

The policy discourse of *Education for citizenship* (NCC, 1990) emerged from a 'general set of Education Reforms designed to create a free market system of education' (Carr, 1991: 382). While bringing improved wealth and prosperity to many of the white majority it also exacerbated economic and structural inequalities for most minority ethnic communities (Gewirtz et al., 1995). The pervasive influence of markets in education and transformation of the discourse of citizenship education into a depoliticized form of political rhetoric was matched with the appearance of a so-called new racism throughout the 1980s (Barker, 1981). This emerged from a long and chequered history of ill-feeling and discrimination (Rex and Moore, 1967; Mullard, 1973), deficit theorizing (Coard, 1971), hostile immigration policies (Patterson, 1963) and deep structural inequalities. Throughout the 1980s 'the "new racism" served to reinforce Powellite[2] views of who was to be included or excluded within a British national identity and provided a rationale for xenophobia and racism towards minorities'(Tomlinson, 2008a: 71). Accordingly, white hegemony (i.e. the ideological dominance of 'whiteness') was allowed to prevail and racism came to be seen as something normal (Taylor, 2009) in a system seeking to control the membership of 'in-groups' and 'out-groups', and thus reinforce a number of potentially damaging hierarchies within education and society.

A radical break with the principles of the welfare state coincided politically with a move towards competitive individualism (Tomlinson, 2008b) and a growing belief in the need to safeguard and protect the British national identity (and white majority) from the 'enemy within'

(Gilroy, 1987). As Ball (2008: 82) suggests, in this climate 'inner cities are represented as a pathological "other" in relation to certain fixed core values', where, for example, the history curriculum became more traditionally British and 'nationalistic' (of which, more later). Such pronouncements were later reinforced through statements like: 'teachers should teach children how to read, not waste their time on the politics of *race*, class and gender' (John Major, cited in Tomlinson, 2008a: 110: emphasis added). As Gillborn (1998: 718) notes 'education reforms of the 1980s and 1990s came increasingly to be characterised by a "de-racialised" discourse that effectively removed ethnic diversity from the agenda and glossed many discriminatory processes'. By the mid-1990s, the non-statutory guidance of *Education for citizenship* (NCC, 1990) had all but disappeared: eclipsed by the hegemony of neo-liberal reform, which served to produce an 'absent presence' (Apple, 1999) of race and ethnicity in education.

Pause and ponder

Market reforms in education have been relentlessly pursued by different governments since 1979. Obtain as much information as you can from newspapers online, looking at the pros and cons of a marketized education system, and answer the following questions:

(1) What are the assumed benefits of the introduction of markets in education?
(2) Which groups within society are markets most likely to benefit and disadvantage?
(3) What are the implications of such market reforms in education for the development of empathy among citizens living in different social and economic conditions?

Policy reincarnation: *Education for citizenship and the teaching of democracy in schools* (Crick Report)

This historical analysis usefully maps the descent of citizenship education, reflecting the status of 'race' and multicultural politics within the 'policyscape' (Ball, 1999), leading up to the beginning of the Crick

(QCA, 1998) era under New Labour. The change of government in 1997 and installation of 'third-way' (Giddens, 1998) thinking brought new hope of a radical shift towards the politics of inclusion and social justice, in particular the possibility of 'developing palliatives to mitigate disadvantage' (Tomlinson, 2008b: 91). However, the discourse of inclusion was tempered by a contradictory and altogether more performative régime, with more exacting standards and pervasive micro-politics of surveillance, including forms of self-policing (Foucault, 1988). Here, citizens are to assume responsibility for their own social, moral and economic welfare and community involvement, through the new mixed economy of positive welfare (Jerome, 2009) and political technologies of 'civility and decency' (Pykett, 2007: 305). The emphasis on the performative and managerial technologies of control in this process illustrates the constraints under which various members of the hand-picked Advisory Board were apparently operating. Thus, any move perceived to 'rock the boat' and undermine the contrived neutrality of the Report and its fixed core values was strictly not an option (Pykett, 2007: 307), especially when a 'political opportunity . . . had to be seized quickly' and where the absent presence of diversity and anti-racism was acknowledged only many years later (Crick, cited in Kiwan, 2008: xiii–xiv). In this policy context, it is no surprise that the reincarnation of citizenship education through the Crick Report (QCA, 1998), should contain only two paragraphs on multicultural issues (Tomlinson, 2008a), and, significantly, no mention of racism at all. As Osler elaborates, 'the Crick report to some degree reflects, rather than challenges, the institutionalised racism of British society: it characterises minorities as having a deficit; it uses patronising language and stereotypes in its depiction of these groups' (2008: 13). Some of these issues of regulation and 'control' can be illustrated through a detailed analysis of the political formation of the document, drawing insights from two earlier critiques (Garratt and Piper, 2008a; 2010).

A useful starting point is the Advisory Group's assertion that with 'the increasingly complex nature of our society, the greater cultural diversity and the apparent loss of a value consensus . . . Cultural diversity raises the issue of *national identity*' (QCA, 1998: 17: emphasis added). Here,

> . . . the discursive formation and linkage of the terms nation, value consensus and the need to address cultural diversity in the context of

national identity is significant as 'diversity' can be read to imply a 'lack', or otherwise interpreted as a 'persistent anxiety' or 'problem' . . . to be dealt with through a frame of 'ethno-cultural unity'. (Watson, 2000; Osler and Starkey, 2001), (Garratt and Piper, 2010: 45)

The political response to 'restore a sense of common citizenship, including a national identity that is secure enough to find a place for the plurality of nations, cultural and ethnic identity' (QCA, 1998: 17), is significant as an affirmation of 'naturalized' fixed core values. Thus, while a surface reading points to a rhetorical reintroduction of the politics of 'race' (and hence improvement in education), at the same time it appeals to a 'sanitized (white-washed) version of history' (Gillborn, 2009: 52) and majoritarian conception of 'Britishness', prevalent throughout the 1980s and 1990s. This in turn privileges a public discourse of political community and national identity that is suspect on at least two counts. First, by ignoring the theme of racism, the Crick Report (QCA, 1998) is complicit with the continuation of the absent presence of 'race' in education and 'other structural disadvantages which act as a key barrier to full and equal citizenship' (Osler, 2008: 13). Second, it treats minorities as somewhat 'suspect communities' (Pantazis and Pemberton, 2009) of the 'enemy within' (Gilroy, 1987): to be held apart from the white majority and challenged on their right to belong as legitimate members of the political state. The tendency towards deficit theorizing in Crick can be found elsewhere within the report's discursive formation. For example, in the statement: 'a more plural approach to racial *disadvantage* requires forms of citizenship which are sensitive to ethnic diversity and offer respect both to individuals and to the social groups to which *they feel they* belong' (QCA, 1998: 17: emphasis added). This formation can

. . . be read to convey an implicit pathology of difference, where the locus of the meaning of 'disadvantage' is entwined with the concept of 'race', which itself is a social construct. Then portrayed as requiring . . . sensitivity or special treatment, ethnic diversity is condemned as the inferior 'other', through the deployment of a notion of belonging that is characterised 'exotic' and which is taken to reside somewhere outside the territory of the authored claim. (Garratt and Piper, 2010: 45)

The persistent 'othering' and implicit condescension and assimilation of minorities within the discourse – against the 'common-sense', invisible perspective of whiteness – is present in the assertion that 'majorities must respect, understand and tolerate minorities . . . minorities must learn and respect the laws, codes and conventions as much as the majority' (QCA, 1998: 18). As Garratt and Piper (2008a: 11) claim:

> . . . critics of this implicit hierarchy (Osler and Starkey, 2001; Hoffman, 2004; Faulks, 2006) note that its condescending tone can be read to imply that minorities are less law-abiding than the dominant white group . . . thus, 'it seems that the dominant group is doing all the teaching and the ethnic minorities all the learning!' (Hoffman, 2004: 267)

In this crucial sense, 'toleration' implies a form of regulation and control: a strong disapproval of behaviour endured by the ruling white majority whose assumed sovereignty can be used to suppress such behaviour if necessary (Modood, 2007). Yet, arguably, integration should always be a two-way process or even a 'multilogical' one (Modood, 2007: 65), that is multi-directional. The rationality and discursive regularity of this 'colour-blind' emphasis is consonant with the 'policyscape' of New Labour, and represents something of a continuation with the past (Tomlinson, 2008a). However, it can be argued that colour-blindness is wholly impotent as a means of promoting social justice since, by definition, this 'prohibits the recognition of particular group identities so that no citizens are treated in a more or less privileged way or divided from each other' (Modood, 2007: 68). Thus, ironically, colour-blind policies that form part of the landscape of liberal politics may actually serve to reinforce and perpetuate existing racial inequalities by placing 'race *equity* at the margins . . . [and] retaining race *injustice* at the centre' (Gillborn, 2009: 65). Consequently, claims about the pedagogical value of political literacy in Crick, to ameliorate the absence of an anti-racist stance (Osler, 2008; Olssen, 2004), seem mildly optimistic. Like its predecessor, the Crick Report neatly (and perhaps even deliberately – cf. Kiwan, 2008) manages to side step such issues and offers no clear guidance for teachers on how to resist the enduring problem of widespread racism. Meanwhile societal ignorance around the politics of 'race' and racism continues unabated amid a smokescreen of performative, managerial and choice-oriented political technologies, and neo-liberal social and education policies (Ball, 2008; Chitty, 2009).

The third coming – *Curriculum review: Diversity and citizenship* (Ajegbo Review) and beyond

At the beginning of the twenty-first century, debates on diversity and citizenship began to increase and intensify in the wake of inter-ethnic disturbances in northern towns in 2001, the 9/11 terrorist attacks in America and London bombings in 2005, with urgent calls for citizenship education to address these issues (Rammell, 2006, cited in Kiwan, 2008). As noted above, the Home Office published a series of reports to address the resulting emergent political themes of community cohesion, diversity and belonging, as well as the need to find a way of reinforcing British values and national identity, while countering the potential threat of terrorist activity (Osler, 2008). As Kiwan (2008: 24) notes, Gordon Brown, then Chancellor of the Exchequer, 'had played a major role in initiating the review . . . and particularly in influencing the framing of its terms of reference'. In 2006, for example, in a speech to the Fabian society on the 'Future of Britishness' Gordon Brown raised the question of what it means to be British in a post-imperial world of plural identities and changing values (Brown, 2006). This followed an earlier appeal in which Brown (2004) questioned the 'core values of Britishness', claiming 'there is a golden thread that runs through British history', comprising 'liberty', 'tolerance' and a 'tradition of fair play'. Going further, in 2007 Jack Straw, then Leader of the House of Commons, claimed that 'we have to be clearer about what it means to be British . . . a "British story" must be at the heart of this' (Straw, 2007).

Given the terms of reference, it is perhaps not surprising that any critical consideration of the concept of 'Britishness' is conspicuously absent in the report of the Ajegbo panel (DfES, 2007). For example, just prior to its publication, Alan Johnson (then Secretary of State for Education) is reported to have 'proposed that schools should focus on "core British values of justice and tolerance"' (cited in Kiwan, 2008: 94), despite otherwise significant concerns regarding the complexity and contested nature of 'Britishness' in relation to matters of 'race'. Moreover, some would say that 'race' itself is an invidious naturalizing concept

(Miles, 1993; Mason, 2000). So, while, more recently, it has become fashionably interchangeable with notions of ethnicity, it remains a socially and politically corrosive concept, 'reflecting the colonial roots of Britain's immigration experience' (Mason, 2006: 105). Accordingly, 'over time the term Britishness has come to mean . . . different things to different people . . . identities are typically constructed as multiple and plural. Throughout our consultations, concerns were expressed, however, about defining "Britishness", about the term's divisiveness and how it can be used to exclude others' (DfES, 2007: 8). In the context of government ministers' political exhortations, the discourse is revealing for its tendency to 'speak' commonsense (white-sense?) to 'race' through an 'unwillingness to name the contours of racism' (Leonardo, 2000: 32, cited in Gillborn, 2009: 54) embedded in the discourse of 'Britishness'. Thus, while extending beyond the narrow colonialism of Crick, the Ajegbo Report (DfES, 2007) nevertheless fails to engage with the pervasive problem of colour-blindness, beneath a veil of liberal democracy. This irony is further compounded by the assertion that 'issues of identity and diversity are more often than not neglected in Citizenship education' (ibid.: 7) and 'tend not to be linked explicitly enough to political understanding' (ibid.: 8). In conflating and further sanitizing the discursive relations of raced inequities and common values and goals, the panel can be found guilty of breaking its own injunction. This is most surprising given the key findings of the Maylor et al. (2007) review – (intended to support the Diversity and Citizenship Curriculum Review Group), which found that:

> . . . in order to effectively acknowledge diversity in Britain, the curriculum needs to provide discursive resources to promote 'collective identities' *and to challenge ideologies that construct the nation and national identity in ways that exclude minority ethnic groups.* (ibid.: 1: emphasis added)

For example, if it is important that young people are enabled to 'consider issues that have shaped the development of UK society – and to understand them through the lens of history' (DfES, 2007: 8), this would surely show that the politics of 'race' and histories of racism (Taylor, 2009) have been repeatedly overlooked in the reimagining of 'Britishness' and citizenship education.

This question encourages further critical analysis of the link between Ajegbo (DfES, 2007) and the wider historical context in which such tensions and regulatory policy discourses have emerged. The appeal to debate around notions of 'Britishness' as a means to resurrect a 'British story' (Straw, 2007), or the 'golden thread that runs through British history' (Brown, 2004) is dubiously melancholic (Gilroy, 2004), but also highly pertinent to the development of a fourth strand for citizenship education. To this, there are three components: 'critical thinking about ethnicity, religion and "race"', an explicit link to political issues and values and the use of contemporary history in teachers' pedagogy to illuminate thinking about contemporary issues relating to citizenship' (DfES, 2007: 12). Politically, the inclusion of 'critical thinking' in the Review usefully encourages the possibility of opening up the discourse of citizenship to enable an interrogation of Britishness and nationalism as otherwise conflated concepts. In terms of educational improvement, this might allow an acknowledgement of 'Otherness' and further develop a more cosmopolitan conception of national identity as 'essential difference' (Pykett, 2007: 310), counting beyond the binary of two: majority/minority. Disappointingly, however, the discourse forecloses prematurely on the possibilities for examining ethnicity and 'race' by twice displacing (and subordinating) the concepts: 'issues of ethnicity and "race", while often controversial, are more often addressed than issues relating to religion' (DfES, 2007: 7, 84). Instead, the review runs the risk of trivializing the issues, by suggesting that 'pupils should have the opportunity to celebrate and embrace diversity' (ibid.: 106), much in the way that multiculturalism was criticized by anti-racist commentators in the 1980s for its perceived flagrant tokenism (Troyna, 1993). Ironically, elsewhere we are reminded that 'myths and stereotypes are still around' (DfES, 2007: 26), that 'there is evidence that issues of "race" and diversity are not always high on schools' agendas' (ibid.: 34), and, further, that 'there is insufficient training for teachers to feel confident with issues of identity [and] "race"' (ibid.: 67). Indeed, if critical thinking on such matters of 'race' and ethnicity is to amount to anything more than mere political rhetoric, then the absence of any articulation of what constitutes criticality in this regulatory context is highly dubious. More so perhaps, given that teachers are widely reported to lack confidence in the area and where such issues have been a low priority in many schools;

less so perhaps in the context of 'the revised QCA Programme of Study at KS3 and KS4 [which] does not contain any explicit reference to anti-racism' (Kiwan, 2008: 94).

Pause and ponder

. . . virtually every major public policy meant to improve race equity has arisen *directly* from resistance and protest by Black and other minoritized communities. Indeed, some of the most significant changes have come about as the result of blood shed. (Gillborn, 2005: 486)

(1) What role might education play in the process of changing and thus improving this situation in the future?
(2) What needs to be done to improve teachers' confidence in tackling issues of 'race' and ethnicity in the classroom in order to bring about change?

With respect to the improvement and future development of education and society, the tensions of our historical past may be productively employed to develop points of resistance and challenge the absent presence of race in citizenship education. Indeed, this is something that Maylor et al. (2007: 1) suggest in as much as citizenship education 'should allow national identity and historical events to be "retold" in order to demonstrate the contribution of minority ethnic groups to British society'. In the context of the Home Office initiatives noted above, it was disappointing that the idea to 'introduce a fourth "pillar" to the citizenship education curriculum on "British social and cultural history"' (Kiwan, 2008: 70), was ultimately rejected. One might question, for example, why it is that under New Labour, Gordon Brown's (2006) commitment to 'liberty', 'tolerance' and a 'tradition of fair play', as the self-styled trinity of 'white civilizing values' (Gillborn, 2009: 51) underpinning British society, sits at odds with Britain's racist past. For the so-called golden thread running through British history glosses all forms of protest and resistance through a discursive naturalization and reification of majoritarian assumptions. As Kymlicka notes 'politics is almost always a matter of both identities and interests. The question is always *which* identities and interests are being promoted?' (Kymlicka, 2002: 328), and so there is always a controlling element. In this case it is a form of politics defining a liberal context in which the 'naturalized' discourse of a 'tradition of fair play' (and hence model for social justice) is effectively displaced as the 'state unavoidably promotes certain cultural identities, and thereby disadvantages others' (Kymlicka, 1995: 108). As Osler suggests:

> The message for educators and the wider public, as reflected in the media, is that Britishness and the British story need to be framed within narrow territorial boundaries. Outsiders need to learn British history in order to integrate into the community of the nation. British history is presented as a single, unproblematic narrative, rather than a complex process, reflecting the various stories and perspectives of Britain as a 'community of communities'. (2009: 92)

The importance of such narrow interests and identities can be illustrated through Jack Straw's (2007) tendency towards 'pathological nostalgia' (Gilroy, 2004), in which he argues that within the concept of British nationality:

> . . . there is room for multiple and different identities, but there has to be a contract that they will not take precedence over the core democratic values of freedom, fairness, tolerance and plurality that define what it means to be British. It is the bargain and it is nonnegotiable.

In a sense, there is nothing inherently British about such values, which simply represent international human rights principles (Osler, 2009). Yet, ironically, the evolving heritage of multicultural Britain appears to have been erased through the telling of a single 'British story', where 'national identity' under New Labour came to mean 'beyond ethnicity' and/or standing outside 'minority' and 'other' (Mirza, 2007). This served to reinforce the combined effect of the demand for tighter immigration controls (Londinium, 2008) – especially against asylum seekers – and 'more exacting' British citizenship tests, to allow immigrants to demonstrate 'commitment' and 'prove integration into communities' (BBC, 2008). It is also contradictory and at odds with what is known culturally and politically and legalistically, for example, the way in which 'dominant narratives have often rendered aspects of the past (even the recent past) invisible to contemporary eyes' (Osler, 2009, 97). Consider, for example, New Labour's commissioning of the Macpherson Inquiry into institutionalized racism, which, while paving the way for the legal amendment of the Race Relations Act 2000, is still not always fully observed in practice. It has, for example, taken the Lawrence family until 2011, 18 years after their son Stephen was brutally murdered, to achieve a semblance of justice in the English legal system through a forthcoming re-trial of the alleged assailants.

From citizenship in schools to the 'Big Society': Old wine in new bottles?

A key change in the development of policy for citizenship education from the latter years of the New Labour administration into the Conservative/Liberal Democrat Coalition Government, is the recognition that citizenship, delivered as a taught subject in schools, has been largely unsuccessful (Garratt and Piper, 2008a; 2008b; 2010). In many ways, however, this is hardly surprising, for citizenship (beyond any legal entitlement), the notion of 'belonging' (Osler and Starkey, 2005) or a sterile conception of 'civics' have long been conceived as a form of social practice. This can be traced back to the Ancient Greek philosophy of Socrates and Aristotle, but also found in more contemporary writing of the twentieth and twenty-first century. John Dewey ([1916] 2007), for example, was fully committed to the idea of participatory democracy and argued that education was not merely preparation for 'life' beyond school, but rather an intrinsic part of life itself. Indeed, education was intended to foster in young people a certain sensitivity towards social and cultural issues through their active engagement and experience, and thus through a process of learning by doing, extending out into the community and across the life course. In this regard, the idea of the 'Big Society' is hardly anything more than very 'old wine' rebottled and rebranded.

In recent policy discourses, the 'Big Society' has been transported from schools to other institutions within society, for example, through active citizenship in prisons. Justice Secretary Ken Clarke has recently stated:

> currently many people in prison are not encouraged to take responsibility and are compelled to live a life of 'enforced, bored idleness'. The Prison Reform Trust report demonstrates that encouraging active citizenship in prisons should play an important part in achieving the government's aims for a 'rehabilitation revolution' and developing the wider concept of the Big Society. (Ken Clarke cited in Prison Reform Trust, 2011)

Much like the appropriation of policy for citizenship education noted above, the question of whether 'active citizenship' actually serves to 'improve' or 'impair' education is a contested argument. On the one hand, such pronouncements appear to provide opportunities for self-improvement beyond the baseline malaise of 'bored idleness', but on the other there are clear regulatory overtones in which active citizenship is exploited as a device to achieve the government's aims for a 'rehabilitation revolution', decoded as enhanced social control. Elsewhere, similar ambiguities can be found in the recent discussion paper *Positive for Youth – Young People's Involvement in Decision Making* (DfE, 2011a). In this, the government is intending to provide funding as a means to enhance young people's participation in decision making:

> [the paper] focuses on the more formal mechanisms through which young people engage with public decision making and democratic processes, and provides 'youth scrutiny', both nationally and locally. Whilst teenagers are the main focus, the paper recognises that the principles that underpin this commitment apply across a much wider age range. Schools also have an important role but it is for them and their governing bodies to decide what arrangements for pupil voice are in place – this funding is primarily intended to support out-of-school participation and decision making. (DfE, 2011a: 1)

Similar to the way that active citizenship is currently being promoted in prisons, this chapter conveys a somewhat ambiguous message concerning issues of 'voice', participation and autonomy. The discussion paper connotes a vague notion of participatory democracy through the aim to engage young people 'with public decision making and democratic processes', but then forecloses prematurely on this opportunity by deter-mining the regulatory mechanisms through which such participation can occur, in this case reinforcing the responsibility of schools and governing bodies 'to decide what arrangements for pupil voice are in place'. In many ways this is strongly characteristic of the way in which the Coalition Government has articulated its vision of the 'Big Society' (see also Chapter 3), so that while it is perfectly acceptable or indeed, commendable for people to volunteer to assume responsibility for improving their own local communities, it is a notion that nevertheless produces tacit compliance and hence reinforces social control. For example, under the guise of enhanced local governance:

> . . . we want to give citizens, communities and local government the power and information they need to come together, solve the problems they face and build the Britain they want. We want society – the families, networks, neighbourhoods and communities that form the fabric of so much of our everyday lives – to be bigger and stronger than ever before. (Cabinet Office, 2011)

Here, central government is able to establish the 'conduct of good conduct' (Foucault, 2002) by generating a discourse in which people are responsible both for themselves and others through imposed forms of 'voluntarism' (in reality, coercion) and collective action. However, when thousands of people become actively empowered to protest vigorously against proposed budgetary cuts and job losses, or indeed in relation to the inexorable rise in student fees within higher education, this is not quite what the government has in mind. In such circumstances, it would seem that intelligent participatory democracy, which we would regard as education for social improvement, and which is reflected, for the most part, in such radical forms of political protest, appears at odds with the Coalition Government's prevailing view of active participation.

Furthermore, against the backdrop of an emerging 'Big Society' lies Prime Minister David Cameron's political exhortations regarding the affirmation of a so-called 'muscular liberalism' in the context of citizenship. Here the concept of 'state multiculturalism' is said to have failed for 'it has stopped us from strengthening our collective identity. Indeed it has deliberately weakened it'. Moreover, state multiculturalism has served to entrench the 'idea that we should respect different cultures within Britain to the point of allowing them – indeed encouraging them – to live separate lives, apart from each other and apart from the mainstream' It has been 'manipulated to entrench the right to difference – which is a divisive concept. What we need is the right to equal treatment despite difference' (Cameron cited in Sparrow, 2011). This discourse, in turn, generates two thorny problems. First, it serves to manipulate what counts as liberal politics in contemporary British society, so that while 'collective identity' is positively condoned, 'the right to difference' is actively condemned. Indeed, this argument is virtually identical to that of former Prime Minister Gordon Brown on the issue of 'Britishness', noted above. In reality, 'equal treatment despite difference' serves actively to dismiss the importance of an 'identity-led' politics and politics of recognition (Taylor, 1992), in which equal dignity and equal respect are properly secured. Secondly, the call to 'strengthen our collective identity' appeals to a form of liberal nationalism, which in turn defines the nature of 'in-groups' and 'out-groups' in a way that serves to reinforce the absence of 'race' and ethnic politics in debates about the future of the 'Big Society'. Is the 'Big Society', for example, both big enough and sufficiently just to recognize difference and duly respect it?

Such concerns are consonant with recent research that shows that intending teachers are resistant to 'simple political rhetoric calling for the teaching of Britishness and specific values' (Clemitshaw and Jerome, 2009: 19), and believe that the question of patriotism must 'be classified as rationally unsettled' (Hand and Pearce, 2009: 458). Looking outside the frame of the liberal state, the politics of 'race' and 'multiculturalism is Janus faced: it has both a forward-looking or progressive side and backward looking or conservative side' (Kymlicka, 2002: 368). This latter conception, resonant in the rhetoric of British prime ministers' past and present, is bound up with the sentiment of nationalism and nation building, to return to a golden age of 'old fashioned cultural conservatism' (Kymlicka, 2002). However, as Young (2004: 195–9) reminds us in relation to the idea of community, for which we can also read 'national identity'/'nation':

> The desire for [national identity] relies on the same desire for social wholeness and identification that underlies racism and ethnic chauvinism on the one hand and political sectarianism on the other . . . the project of the ideal [nation] as the radical other of existing society denies difference in

the sense of the contradictions and ambiguities of social life . . . no telos of the final society exists.

Ultimately, we suggest that unless there is a radical shift in, and reprioritization of, the politics of education policy and practice it is doubtful any putative system of the future will lead to genuine social improvement. Thus, while we acknowledge that the right to difference, equal dignity and equal respect within a participatory democratic framework are the essential prerequisites of any 'good' liberal education, and hence education for improvement, we must remind ourselves that 'education cannot compensate for society' (Bernstein, 1968). Indeed, the chances of it doing so seem only remotely possible if education policy and practice are able to become authentically self-critical, democratic and more than a means to instrumental, short-term regulatory aims and purposes.

Notes

1 Parts of this analysis have been reproduced with permission from Taylor and Francis publishers from the original article: Garratt, D. (2011) 'Equality, difference and the absent presence of "race"', in Citizenship Education in the UK, *London Review of Education*, 9(1): 27–39.

2 Reference to the 'Rivers of Blood' speech, by Enoch Powell at the meeting of the Conservative Association, 20 April 1968.

Further reading

Gillborn, D. (2009) 'Education policy as an act of white supremacy', in E. Taylor, D. Gillborn and G. Ladson-Billings (eds) *Foundations of Critical Race Theory in Education*, London: Routledge (pp.51–69).

Gilroy, P. (1987) *There ain't no Black in the Union Jack*, London: Hutchinson.

Modood, T. (2007) *Multiculturalism*, Cambridge: Polity.

Race, R. (2011) *Multiculturalism and Education*, London: Continuum.

White, J. (1982) *The Aims of Education Restated*, London: Routledge.

Policy and Social Justice

Chapter Outline

Introduction

This chapter examines education policies in Britain in relation to social justice. In doing so, the chapter draws attention to the competing aims of education and tensions evident in a number of policy areas. The chapter begins by exploring the different dimensions of the concept of social justice and considers three discernable philosophical traditions that inform political thinking and aspirations in Westernized countries namely, liberal-humanist, market-individualistic and social-democratic. Social justice in education necessitates that *access* to the same quality of educational processes should be *equitable*, even if there are unequal outcomes as a consequence. To this endeavour, the chapter explores the tensions manifested in specific education policies of the Conservative, New Labour and Conservative/Liberal Democrat Coalition Governments. First of all, the social democratic post-war settlement of the mid-1940s with the creation of the welfare state is considered and also how this underwent radical reform under the Conservative administration of Margaret Thatcher. The education system was just one aspect of the welfare state that was reformed and which further established the foundation for subsequent legislation in successive Conservative, New Labour and Conservative/Liberal Democrat Coalition Governments. The introduction of a range of measures and initiatives by the Thatcher Government, which culminated in the ERA of 1988, transformed the education system so that it was seen in terms of a market. The producers of education, that is, schools, colleges and universities, have since operated in a competitive environment providing, in theory, greater diversity and choice (see, for example, Chapter 6). An analysis of the impact of marketization and privatization of education policy post-1979 to the present reveals tensions between the political discourses of social democracy and the New Right in relation to the competing aims of equity and inclusion. The chapter examines policy convergences, continuities, overlaps and differences between the policy approaches of successive governments. We suggest the move, by successive governments in the United Kingdom, to drive up standards and achieve excellence has produced a series of largely unsatisfactory policy composites (Ball, 2008).

The dimensions of social justice

We begin this chapter by exploring the meaning of social justice. Not unlike many other concepts, it has different connotations, is a contested phrase and is politically malleable. The concept typically applies to all aspects of social life and is one where there is social, economic and political (including legal) equity. While a socially just society may be an ideal aspiration, a comparative and international analysis reveals that it is impossible to provide a unified definition because social justice is expressed differently across different nations and cultural traditions (Rizvi, 2009). However, injustice is more readily universally recognizable and has 'material reality' as (Rizvi, 2009: 91–2) indicates:

> Those who are hungry or poor, or homeless, do not need abstract philosophical discussions in order to realize that they are subjected to marginalization, discrimination and oppression. The idea of justice thus points to something real and tangible, and represents a moral blight on communities that do not attempt to do their best to mitigate its worst effects.

In most Westernized countries, over recent decades, social justice aspirations influenced by the distributive paradigm have featured in political thinking. While particular local and historical circumstances, cultural traditions, social movement activism and political aspirations impact on the nature of social justice, three distinct philosophical traditions informed by the distributive paradigm are apparent: liberal-humanist, market-individualistic and social-democratic. These are now discussed in turn.

The liberal-humanist tradition is associated primarily with Rawls' (1999) basic principles, as conceptualized in his *A Theory of Justice* originally published in 1971. Although Rawls (ibid.) does not utilize the term a great deal in his work, his ideas about social justice have come to dominate contemporary understandings (Wolff, 2008). Rawls (1999: 53) outlines the two principles as follows:

> First: each person is to have an equal right to the most extensive scheme of equal basic liberties compatible with a similar scheme of liberties for others.
>
> Second: social and economic inequalities are to be arranged so that they are both (a) reasonably expected to be to everyone's advantage, and (b) attached to positions and offices open to all.

The first is the 'liberty principle' and the second actually comprises two parts; (a) is the 'difference principle' and (b) the 'fair opportunity principle'. Rawls' (ibid.) principles encompass notions of fairness and individual freedom in addition to the state's responsibility to create policies and interventions that facilitate access, equity and participation and eliminate barriers arising from inequitable power relations. It is the difference principle that is closest to traditional notions of social justice and is Rawls' particular contribution to the debate (Wolff, 2008). Chapman and West-Burnham (2010) take this a step further conceptualizing a socially just society as that which achieves 'well-being' for all its citizens. As such, they offer the following description:

> In very practical terms a society committed to social justice would ensure that every child grows up experiencing the optimum levels of well-being . . . A socially just society ensures that every child, irrespective of social background, parentage, post code or any variable, has an entitlement in

terms of equality and equity to the benefits of growing up in a modern, democratic and affluent society. (Chapman and West-Burnham, 2010: 29–30)

It is not the aim here to attempt to provide a definitive conceptualization of social justice, for there are many diverse viewpoints and social justice has varied and disparate uses. Before moving on to consider market-individualism and social-democratic traditions, it is useful at this point to consider what typically lies at the heart of social justice for citizens. Contemporary scholars often consider its focus as egalitarian and entailing citizens having an equal share in terms of access to and distribution of resources, entitlement, representation and also having a 'voice'. Young's (1990) articulation of the 'distributive paradigm' relates to the way in which material and non-material goods and resources are distributed in society; basically, how much people get. It would follow then that a just society constitutes one that distributes its goods and resources (and burdens) fairly. When equity is realized, then justice is achieved. Many contemporary scholars who write about social justice (e.g. Miller, 1999) equate social justice with distributional justice (Boyles et al., 2009). In considering the different dimensions of social justice Gewirtz (1998) raises some important issues, particularly in relation to distributive justice. She explores the different facets of social justice and makes a distinction between its distributional and relational dimensions. Gewirtz (1998: 472) purports that distributive justice has tended to be conceived in two ways: first, in terms of *equality of opportunity,* noted as the 'traditional "weak" liberal definition of justice' and secondly, as *equality of outcome,* which is the 'more radical "strong" liberal version of justice'. While equality of opportunity refers to equal formal rights, access and participation, equality of outcome is different in that it seeks to ensure, through interventionist policies, to combat disadvantage and maintain equal rates of success for different societal groups. However, Gewirtz (ibid.) argues this is a somewhat narrow conception of justice, which needs to be expanded upon. Thus, she suggests a distinction is made between the distributive and the *relational* dimensions of justice. Relational justice constitutes the nature of the relationships that structure society and which Gewirtz (ibid.) regards as being 'strongly connected' to, though 'separate' from, the distributive dimension. Her explanation of the relational dimensions is, in essence, about issues of power:

> It is about the *nature* and *ordering* of social relations, the formal and informal rules which govern how members of society treat each other both on a macro level and at a micro interpersonal level. Thus it refers to the practices and procedures which govern the organization of political systems, economic and social institutions, families and one-to-one social relationships. These things cannot unproblematically be conceptually reduced to matters of distribution. (Gewirtz, 1998: 471)

Gerwitz (ibid.) contends the distributional dimension is individualistic in nature whereas the relational dimension is holistic and more concerned with 'the nature of inter-connections between individuals in society'. At this point, it is useful to give consideration to what might be considered the antithesis of social justice, namely inequality. Inequalities exist in many forms in society in the United Kingdom and are based on, for example, social class, gender, race, ethnicity and physical ability. Inequalities are produced and re-produced in different ways and at different times and, in recent times, often as a result of post-welfarist[1] policies, the restructuring of public services and changes in government and/or as a result of the global economy impacting on national decision-making. Significantly, however, inequalities are manifested at different times in the range of concerns identified by policy-makers and in the formation of different understandings of what is deemed as 'problematic'. As such, the concept of social justice is not necessarily fixed or static and has seen notable shifts since the creation of the welfare state in the United Kingdom in the post-war settlement of the mid-1940s. Phillips (1997: 143), for example, notes a shift in the nature of the language used to talk about social justice issues from the early 1980s onwards noting 'difference in particular seems to have displaced inequality as the central concern of political and social theory'. The focus on 'difference', belonging, for example, to a particular gender or ethnic group, is currently given more attention by policy-makers and, as such, has led to 'politics of difference' (Harvey, 1993; Leonard, 1997).

The social democratic settlement pursued social justice based on redistribution from the mid-1940s to the late 1970s, when thinking shifted towards individual rights and to market-individualism. This perspective rests on the idea of what people deserve rather than on the notion of fairness per se. It operates on the assumption that the state does not have the right to transfer goods or property owned by individuals without their consent. Thus the market is perceived as a neutral mechanism in facilitating social exchange and the exercise of individual choice. In contrast, the social-democratic tradition rejects the notion of individualism while promoting that of community. Also, the idea of the *laissez-faire* market sits uneasy with the social democratic view and justice, unless markets are controlled to ensure equal treatment, access, participation in decision-making and in power relations. Different governments in the United Kingdom since 1945 have emphasized different aspects of these traditions of social justice. These shifts in emphasis are now pursued.

Pause and ponder

(1) What is your understanding of social justice?

(2) If possible, ask someone else their understanding of social justice. Are your views different? If so, how?

(3) Different educational systems address social justice in different ways. In your opinion, how and to what extent should education be structured as an instrument for promoting social justice?

The construction of welfare

In the mid-1940s, in the aftermath of the Second World War, the universalist welfare state was created in Britain to provide assistance for all citizens and offered protection from 'the cradle to the grave'. The state directly intervened in what became known as the 'post-war social settlement' or the 'social democratic consensus' to address society's five perceived social 'evils', namely, want, squalor, idleness, ignorance and disease (Williams, 1989). What is evident in this era is a political discourse of social democracy with a positive concern for social justice and various policies, initiatives and interventions that were deemed to be equitable, designed to achieve equality and eliminate poverty. There was a consistent expansion of welfare through social policies from 1945 until the mid-1970s (Jones, 1991; Sullivan, 1992), which was underpinned by a Keynesian approach to the economy (see Chapter 6). Education was regarded as the means by which society's inequalities and problems could be tackled and bring about social change and a socially just society. Educational initiatives were framed by the language (discourse) of 'equality of opportunity' whereby, regardless of social class, family background or location every child was to have educational opportunities via the tripartite system that emanated from the 1944 Education Act (see Chapter 4). Higher education also expanded with the introduction of grants for students and the growth of provision for teacher education. As a means of combating social and economic deprivation policies such as free school meals came into being for disadvantaged children as well as free milk at school for all children (David, 1980). The prevalence of the post-war social democratic ideology entailed creating more socially just educational policies and practices.

By the mid- to late 1970s, however, the welfare state was considered inherently inefficient, monopolistically bureaucratic and a tremendous drain on resources, which could not be sustained (Sullivan, 1994). In addition, there was growing disillusionment with education as a mechanism for promoting equality of opportunity. The massive investment in education following the social democratic consensus on education policy was considered very expensive while standards remained poor (Batho, 1990). Added to this there was teacher unrest between 1968 and 1974 (Grace, 1987). These events were significant in marking a turning point in attitudes towards education and also in the politicization of educational issues. In this climate of economic decline education, along with all other public services such as health care, housing and social services, came under increasing scrutiny.

The New Right and the reconstruction of welfare

The Conservative party, under the leadership of Margaret Thatcher, came into government in 1979 by which time the welfare state in Britain was thought by policy-makers to be in crisis. Confidence in the system had deteriorated with the onset of economic problems following the world oil crisis of 1973. The rate of economic growth was curtailed as investments and profits fell, unemployment increased and the economy contracted in the mid-1970s. Advocates of the New Right (see Chapter 1) used the economic problems to challenge the post-war social settlement and the symbolic place of the welfare state within it (Clarke and Newman, 1997). New Right ideology, coalescing neo-liberal and neo-conservative philosophies, challenged the supremacy of the welfare state and became a dominant force in policy. Neo-liberal economics emphasized the primacy of markets, free from state interference, as more effective mechanisms for the distribution of social resources. This philosophy presupposes that the privatization of public services and a reduction in the role of the state would alleviate the burden of public expenditure as the state's bureaucratic structures impeded Britain's economic survival and needed to be dismantled. Competition, it was argued, would increase the efficiency of public sector organizations and offer individuals freedom of choice. Incorporated in New Right politics is a neo-conservative strand committed to the regeneration of traditional moral values, authority, the virtues of a strong state and intervention of the government to achieve these (King, 1987; Gamble, 1988; Tomlinson, 1993). Whether complementary or contradictory, neo-liberal and neo-conservative philosophies came together under Thatcherism.

The New Right philosophy was essentially constructed around three key issues. First, the welfare state was regarded as expensive and a major factor contributing to the country's economic decline. Public expenditure on personal social services, health, housing, social security and education, for example, was viewed as a colossal drain on resources that could not be sustained. There was a very heavy burden on the citizen, as taxpayer, and this conflicted with the Conservative's commitment to low rates of direct taxation. Secondly, public services were considered inefficient and bureaucratic and the citizen, as consumer, was being denied effective choice of service provision. Thirdly, the effects of state welfare encouraged a disincentive to work and undermined individualism and initiative. The citizen being dependent on welfare services in a 'benefits culture' was thus deemed a 'scrounger', receiving public handouts to evade responsibility (Williams, 1989; Sullivan, 1994). New Right ideology perceived that the privatization of such services and a reduction in the role of the state would alleviate the burden of public expenditure, increase their efficiency and offer freedom of choice to citizens. These three issues constitute different strands of the New Right ideology: a neo-liberal strand stressing the superiority of markets as more effective mechanisms for the distribution of social resources and the revival of economic individualism; and a neo-conservative strand committed to the revitalization of traditional morality and social authority (Clarke and Newman, 1997).

Margaret Thatcher, as prime minister, pursued the ideas and ideology of the New Right, which fundamentally reconstructed the relationship between the state and social welfare. Thatcherite individualism can be summarized as the belief that it is more preferable for people to look after themselves (and their families) than for them to combine as a society to provide for themselves collectively (Rentoul, 1990). This is best illustrated in Margaret Thatcher's classic and widely quoted statement:

> There's no such thing [as society]. There are individual men and women, and there are families and no government can do anything except through people and people look to themselves first. It is our duty to look after ourselves. (Keay, 1987: 8–10)

The ideology of individualism was coupled with the strategy of successive governments from 1979 to transform British society and its values, and to eliminate socialism. Subsequently, competitive markets increasingly became a more prominent feature in the welfare state during the 1980s with internal (or quasi) markets and competition introduced into the public sector. This was most visible in the health and education services. The government's attempt to reduce expenditure was not entirely successful however, and it actually increased by 11 per cent in real terms between 1979 and 1990 (Johnson, 1990). This was mainly due to increased social security expenditure as a result of rising unemployment and the need to finance the government's tougher policy on law and order and defence. Fundamental changes took place in all aspects of social policy, which led to legislation through major Acts of Parliament. A common factor throughout all areas of social policy was the belief in markets and competition.

The education marketplace: From equality to quality

The adoption of neo-liberal policies and a minimal state resulted in schools, colleges and universities having to operate in a more competitive environment. The chapter concentrates only on policies for schools, however, to illustrate how legislation, notably the ERA and subsequent policies by the New Labour Government, encouraged schools to compete for a limited number of pupils in a market environment. The Conservative policies were deliberate attempts to provide greater diversity and choice by making schools significantly different from each other; new types of institutions emerged after 1988. City Technology Colleges (CTCs), private schools with a vocational orientation that encouraged pupils to seek future careers in science or technology, were set up (the original intention was they would be sponsored by businesses). Grant-maintained Schools, which could opt out of LEA control, were also created. These new institutions provided diversity in the system as well as reintroducing selective education. Open enrolment and parental choice became the main determinants of school admissions during the 1980s and the introduction of a range of measures, such as national assessment and performance/league tables, transformed the education system by introducing market forces. Through the Assisted Places Scheme the government covered, in part or fully, tuition fees for 'the most able' pupils to attend schools in the independent rather than maintained sector.

It is claimed that marketization produces a system more responsive to customer requirements, providing greater diversity between schools and thus greater choice for parents. It is at this juncture that we can see a fundamental shift from the traditional ways of thinking about social justice in education (i.e. the social democratic approach that underpinned post-war policies until the 1980s) with a strong role for the state in realizing greater equality of access, opportunities and outcomes. Hereafter, education is regarded as a commodity with schools, as rival outlets, competing for parents' custom, and parents henceforth empowered to choose from a range of products. The beginnings of the break-up of state provision and the push for privatization can be seen. Through the

Local Management of Schools (LMS) schools were empowered, for example, to manage their own budget, set their own expenditure and contract services from outside the LEA. New school types were established that could be taken over and run by businesses (CTCs) and the Nursery Voucher Scheme enabled parents to choose from a range of pre-school provision and 'spend' their entitlement in state or private nurseries (Ball, 2007).

Proponents of the market ideology argue that all parents should have the right to send their children to the school of their choice (not just the geographically nearest one) as this will enable individual aspirations to be aligned with anticipated school outcomes (Braithwaite, 1992). The state's role and responsibility in such a process is no longer that of provider of a common education service for all children (Pring, 1986), but a role that ensures parents have the right to individual choice of school under free market conditions (Braithwaite, 1992). Advocates of neo-liberalism contend that competition among schools will ultimately raise standards in education, improve quality and provide accountability through the mechanism of market forces. The free market ideology supposes that by encouraging diversity and choice a more competitive environment will be created between producers. The right of choice in education has been given in law to parents, empowering them as consumers of education. Implicit in this process is the assumption that given adequate information parents, as consumers, will make rational choices.

Neo-liberalism presents the market as neutral and all consumers having a viable choice. Parents have been regarded collectively as a homogeneous group of consumers in the education market, with an interest in their child's education. This ideology presupposes that all parents have the resources available to them to facilitate choice: the time to travel in search of the most appropriate school for their child, the availability of cars to transport their child over any distance, the resources to fund public transport and, in the last resort, the capacity to move house. It presupposes that by using indicators of performance such as league tables of national examinations, obtaining prospectuses and visiting schools the role of parents, as clients or consumers of education, is to make considered and informed choices on behalf of their children (Angus, 1994). However, the lived experience of choice reveals the complexity and injustice of the education market, as Ranson (1993: 337) strongly contests:

> Choice imposes costs which are likely to be prohibitive for many families. As emerging evidence indicates, for many families, certainly in rural areas, the promise of choice is regarded cynically as empty rhetoric. To lack resources is to be disenfranchised from the polity of the market.

The political rhetoric strongly emphasizes increased parental choice. However, largely due to economic or geographical differences, parents do not have available to them, or experience, the same range of choices. In reality, the concept of 'choice' constitutes different meanings to different groups of families and is socially and culturally constructed (Carroll and Walford, 1997). Research conducted on the issue of parental choice suggests that certain types of parents have a greater capacity than others to 'play the market' and are more inclined to make a proactive choice (Ball et al., 1995; Gewirtz et al., 1994; 1995). Parents possessing the appropriate 'cultural capital' (Bourdieu and Passeron, 1990) necessary to play the system are more likely to succeed in the education market, making informed choices and securing places for their children in more reputable and advantaged schools. Children from disadvantaged backgrounds, whose parents possess inadequate knowledge of the education system and the choice mechanisms of the education market, are more likely to end up in schools with insufficient facilities and of inferior academic performance (Gewirtz et al., 1994; 1995; Carroll and Walford, 1997). Researchers have examined the socio-economic inequalities of choice, categorized parents according to the extent to which they participate in the education marketplace and correlated this to their social class. Parents have been labelled as 'choosers' and 'non-choosers', (Adler et al., 1989), 'alert' and 'inert' (Willms and Echols, 1992), 'privileged', 'semi-skilled' and the 'disconnected' (Ball et al., 1995) and 'active' and 'passive' (Carroll and Walford, 1997). These dualisms and categorizations illustrate different responses to choice by middle- and working-class parents. Arguably, this form of school admissions system does not adequately address issues relating to equity and social justice and is a clear departure from the 'earlier implicit consensus commitment to social justice' (Jonathan cited in West, 2006: 15).

Market-individualism is not unique to the United Kingdom however, but emerged due to the global propensity for and convergence towards neo-liberal thinking in education (see Chapters 5, 6 and 8). Nevertheless, the Conservative Government set the stage for a continuation of neo-liberal marketization and greater privatization.

New Labour: An intense phase of educational policy-making

New Labour positioned its ideological thinking as 'the Third Way' (Giddens, 2000), a perspective which harnesses a social capitalist model (state intervention) and a neo-liberal model (market forces) to create social and economic well-being (see Chapter 1). The New Labour Government was committed to the market model and to social justice, but arguably Third Way philosophy is primarily concerned with inclusion rather than equality. Where citizens were 'socially excluded' New Labour saw it was the state's responsibility to step in albeit to assist in restoring self-sufficiency rather than creating dependency. Government priorities changed under New Labour with resources targeted towards disadvantaged communities through social security and investment in public services (Driver, 2008). New Labour placed education at the heart of its policies and as a mechanism for change that would alleviate social exclusion and bring about equality of opportunity (Hall and Raffo, 2009). Significantly, New Labour regarded educational qualifications as a route out of poverty and targeted resources at those from socio-economically disadvantaged backgrounds. New Labour thus invested heavily in education to drive their policies via intervention and direction while simultaneously regarding education as 'the best economic policy there is' (Blair, 1996: 66) (see Chapter 6).

According to Exley and Ball (2011: 110) 'New Labour took the Conservative infrastructure and gave it meat and teeth'. Few outright policy reversals were made and were designed 'to benefit the many, not just the few', notably the abolition of the Nursery Voucher and Grant-maintained Schools and phasing out the Assisted Places Scheme. The education market remained, as did the mechanism of 'choice'; thus, the inevitable reproduction of the inequities of neo-liberalism (as described above) continued. Perhaps the most notable difference of the incoming New Labour Government was its reluctance to rely merely on market forces to improve quality and raise standards in schools, but to intervene directly into the curriculum and school organization and by setting challenging targets for pupil and student achievement. New Labour was not averse to the private sector or the involvement of business in providing core educational services and policy delivery. LMS was maintained, which further weakened local education authorities, but central control and direction increased. Like its Conservative predecessor, the New Labour Government drew attention to failing schools, and pledged there would be 'zero tolerance' of under-performance and 'speedy intervention where necessary':

> when schools fail we will intervene promptly to protect the prospects of the pupils. (Blair, 1998: 30)

Poor performing schools were 'named and shamed' with arrangements made to close them down and re-open with a new head teacher under 'Fresh Start' or, later on, as Academies (independent state secondary schools – of which, more later). Policy-makers proclaimed that 'significant extra resources' would be invested in education; in return 'significant improvements in standards' were expected from school teachers and leaders (DfEE, 1998a: 4). The proposals thus offered 'something for something' (Blunkett, 1998) and investment in education was tied to accountability.

Before considering New Labour's commitment to social justice we first examine what 'old' Labour represented during its periods in the government post-1945 (1945–51, 1964–70 and 1974–79). Old Labour favoured Keynesian demand management whereby the state influenced the direction of the economy (see Chapter 6) underpinned by the philosophy that state planning and investment would maintain full employment. The party also leaned towards state welfarism and a 'tax and spend' approach (Driver and Martell, 1998). Basically, the thinking was that economic growth, as steered by government intervention, would pay for the services of the welfare state, thereby bringing greater equality to society. In addition, there was public ownership (e.g. rail, electricity, gas, telecommunications), controls on private business (e.g. on export of capital) and a strong role for trade unions in the workplace and in the shaping of policy (corporatism). 'New' Labour is significantly different to old Labour in that in the aftermath of the 18 years of Conservative Governments (1979–97) it is associated with: not re-nationalizing privatized industries, not re-establishing controls on business and not re-establishing a strong role for trade unions. However, when Tony Blair became prime minister in 1997 he contended Labour's old values of community, inclusion, fairness and social justice remained the same (Driver and Martell, 1998). As such, New Labour intervened directly in education to tackle social disadvantage and improve the country's economic performance:

> To overcome economic and social disadvantage and to make opportunity a reality . . . To compete in the global economy . . . We must overcome the spiral of disadvantage . . . I ask of you to join us in making the crusade for higher standards a reality in every classroom and every household in the country. (DfEE, 1997a: 3–4)

New Labour's policies were designed to restore social cohesion and social justice, which it perceived as an antidote to the emphasis on the individual and which had emanated through New Right policies. New Labour's development of the concept of 'social exclusion', which it saw as emanating from 'a multiplicity of factors in peoples' lives' (Dyson, et al., 2009: 147), led in turn to a multiplicity of initiatives and signified increased awareness of a way in which certain groups of people, for various reasons, live outside mainstream society; those who are socially marginalized and are disempowered. New Labour aimed to combat social exclusion through its policy initiatives believing the socially excluded are unable to realize their full potential, participate fully in the workings of the institutions that govern peoples' lives or consider themselves full and equal members of the community. In terms of education, New Labour moved away from the notion that educational failure is associated with deprivation and social class position towards the ideas elucidated by the school effectiveness and school improvement research fields; that schools have the potential to make a difference (Reynolds, 1986). Policy-makers, however, have tended to ignore the appeal from school improvement researchers that context-specific improvement strategies are necessary (Harris and Chapman, 2004) and that a one-size-fits-all policy solution is futile. Nevertheless, New Labour invested massively in intervention programmes to support schools in 'challenging circumstances' in order to combat disadvantage. These are too numerous to discuss at length here (see Chapman and Gunter, 2009 for more detail) and so we highlight a selection. The *Excellence in Cities* programme (DfEE, 1997b) provided additional funding for schools in deprived areas, aimed to raise achievement among working-class groups and promote social inclusion (Whitty, 2001). *Education Action Zones* involved business participation and were introduced as part of the School Standards and Frameworks Bill in areas with low levels of educational attainment and where there were high levels of social exclusion. *The Schools in Challenging Circumstances Initiative*, introduced in 2001, and the *National Challenge* in 2008 were initiatives for schools in particularly difficult contexts and failing to meet government floor targets. In order to improve standards they received additional funding and resources, inspection and external support. The focus on urban poverty came with the 2002 City Academies Programme that built on the Conservative's CTCs legacy. When in opposition the Labour party had opposed this policy considering it unjust and inequitable. Nevertheless, when in government, New Labour created City Academies that were independent of LEA control and sponsored by private companies, charities or individuals (Beckett, 2007). An investment of £2 million was initially required towards the new school (though this was later dropped) and an academy created following the closure of a failing secondary school (or several in a locality). Over time, Academies changed (see Gunter, 2010) so that the perquisites of urban, failing and city schools were no longer qualifying attributes and sponsors included faith or voluntary groups, universities and other schools.

   Early Years provision expanded with an increase in places for 3–5 year olds, and greater concentration of resources with the aim of developing high-quality provision to assist the educational development of pre-school children. The *Every Child Matters* (ECM) agenda (DfES, 2004) gave rise to a package of welfare reforms. Its list of five desirable outcomes led to sweeping changes, including inter-agency collaboration, which were legislated in 2004 through the Children's Act. Ambiguities are evident in New Labour's policies as illustrated in ECM. For example, the production of evidence as individual high performing learning organizations in relation to the inter-agency collaboration demanded by ECM, two of the five desired ECM outcomes 'achieving economic well-being' and 'making a positive contribution' sit outside the remit of the newly integrated children's services and it is not clear how the five desired outcomes relate to each other, which to priorities or which services are expected to take the lead. This raises all sorts of questions, especially around accountability and professional boundaries. Which group of professionals are accountable and when? What are the professional territories and boundaries? How can effective collaboration be achieved? These are just some of the ambiguities that those working at the forefront of policy implementation and/or delivery have to reconcile.

Early intervention programmes such as Sure Start, Baby Bonds and increasing childcare places attempted to address inequalities at birth aiming at giving everyone, despite their background, a minimum starting point. Although not equal, this 'asset-based' approach to social justice is one where everyone has 'a fair chance of making the most of their lives given their abilities and effort' (Driver, 2008: 66). However, such policies are problematic as they alone are unlikely to succeed in narrowing the gap in the distribution of wealth and income between rich and poor social groups. While New Labour's policies made some inroads in addressing relative poverty, citizens although granted 'choice' may not necessarily have the capacity or resources to use them. In that sense, despite radical reform of the public sector and record spending British society remained unequal in 2010 when New Labour's time in government came to a close.

> **Pause and ponder**
>
> Economic competition, growth and innovation have powerful effects on social structure and processes of inclusion and exclusion. New Labour placed education at the centre of its policies for encouraging economic growth (see also Chapter 6). Can this be achieved without creating social fragmentation?

Coalition: Convergences, continuities and overlaps?

When the Conservative/Liberal Democrat Coalition entered government in May 2010 it demonstrated, almost immediately, a different emphasis in policy, which was framed by the rhetoric of the

Conservative's 'big society'. This had been alluded to in pre-Coalition days and articulated by David Cameron in 2009:

> We believe that a strong society will solve our problems more effectively than big government has or ever will, we want the state to act as an instrument for helping to create that strong society. Our alternative to big government is the big society . . . The era of big government has run its course. Poverty and inequality have got worse, despite Labour's massive expansion of the state. We need new answers now, and they will only come from a bigger society, not a bigger government. (Gallager, 2009)

The big society embraces the idea that power should reside with individuals, social groups and communities rather than with government and its organizations. Just as 'Thatcherism' and the 'Third Way' evolved as political projects so, inevitably, the notion of the big society will advance or indeed wane given the scale of cuts that the Coalition has imposed, which has significantly weakened confidence in the big society (The Guardian, 2011).

One of the Coalition's first visible changes in education was to scrap the Department for Children Schools and Families (DCSF), which had overseen the integration of services outlined in the previous section, and replace it with the Department for Education (DfE). With the emphasis in education firmly on 'schools' the Coalition intended to facilitate change by removing some of New Labour's regulatory frameworks, reducing unnecessary bureaucracy, giving schools and head teachers greater freedom, promoting diversity and creating greater choice. The focus on schools is hardly surprising given the indications when the Conservatives were in opposition. As the then Shadow Schools Secretary Michael Gove explained how a Conservative Government would narrow the achievement gap:

> The central mission of the next Conservative government is the allevi-ation of poverty and the extension of opportunity. And nowhere is action required more than in our schools. Schools should be engines of social mobility . . . The sad truth about our schools today is that, far from making opportunity more equal, they only deepen the divide between the rich and poor, the fortunate and the forgotten . . . We will break up the bureaucratic monopoly on school provision, which denies

parents choice and introduce competition specifically to help drive up
standards. (Shepherd, 2009)

New types of schools have been proposed and the conditions created for
'Free Schools'. Parents, other groups and private providers are encouraged
to set up and run their own schools; this represents a new policy direction
based on the Swedish model (see Chapter 8), but which also creates
greater fragmentation in the education system. The Conservative/
Liberal Democrat Coalition Government has expanded the academies
programme through the Academies Act 2010 enabling outstanding
schools to apply for academy status as well as extending this to the
primary sector. This remains a contested area of policy (Gunter, 2010).

While in opposition, and losing the General Elections of 2001 and
2005, the Conservatives have had time to contemplate their pre-1997
policy approach and challenge the propensity for New Right theory.
David Cameron's more 'compassionate conservatism' (see Hari, 2010)
with a new focus on social justice takes its influence from the Centre for
Social Justice (see www.centreforsocialjustice.org.uk/). According to
Exley and Ball (2011), the Conservatives see the educational failure so
evident in the attainment gap between the rich and the poor and the
lack of social mobility as issues to be remedied by individuals, families,
communities, social enterprise and the market rather than state
regulation of education. Exley and Ball (ibid.: 113) sum up the current
policy approach in education:

> It is a bricolage of often incoherent international 'borrowings', the input
> of a diverse set of 'think tanks' ranging from the Centre for Social Justice
> through to the Red Conservatism of ResPublica, the takeover of many of
> Labour's 'good ideas', and the underlying tensions of traditionalism ('real'
> subjects) liberalism (school diversity and choice) and economism
> (vocationalism).

The universalism of state education provision was arguably undermined from the 1980s onwards and, arguably, policies have continued
to foster social inequalities. The conception of social justice is such that
public policies are mostly concerned with issues of distribution and
access. So, in terms of education, there is an increased emphasis on

access to education (e.g. widening participation in higher education) and raising standards. However, as educational outcomes and research findings have both shown, these measures do not lead to equity and, as has been illustrated in this chapter, the pursuit of equity does not always appear to be the primary objective of some policies.

Over to you . . .

Understanding the continuities and differences of education policies is an important part of policy analysis. Note down what you think are the key continuities and differences between the education policies of the following governments:

(1) New Labour and Conservative (post-1979)
(2) Conservative/Liberal Democrat Coalition Government and New Labour
(3) Conservative/Liberal Democrat Coalition Government and Conservative (post-1979)
  (a) How do you account for these differences?
  (b) Do you see any particular patterns?

Note

1 Policies that expect the individual to become economically self-sufficient rather than being dependent on state provision.

Further reading

Chapman, C. and Gunter, H.M. (2009) *Radical Reforms: Perspectives on an Era of Educational Change*, Abingdon, Oxen: Routledge.

Driver, S. and Martell, L. (1998) *New Labour: Politics after Thatcherism*, Cambridge: Polity Press.

Exley, S. and Ball, S.J. (2011) 'Something old, something new: understanding Conservative education policy', in H. Bochel (ed.) *The Conservative Party and Social Policy*, Cambridge: Polity Press (pp. 97–117).

Gunter, H.M. (ed.) (2010) *The State and Education Policy: The Academies Programme*, London: Continuum.

The Evolving Primary Curriculum

4

Chapter Outline

Introduction

In state-maintained primary schools teachers in England currently 'deliver' a statutory National Curriculum and pupils are evaluated through national assessment procedures. Over a period of three decades there has been increased emphasis on raising standards, standardization in schools and the development of standardized indicators of performance through tests and examinations. Key Stage Two results (Year 6, final year of primary education) are published in the form of league tables for public scrutiny in England providing 'consumers of education' (i.e. parents, stakeholders and policy-makers) with comparative data. Inevitably, the growing emphasis on output and testing has pressurized teachers, and by default pupils, to focus on performance.

Teaching Assistants and Higher Level Teaching Assistants provide support for teachers within the primary classroom, although their role and the boundaries in which they operate are sometimes ambiguous and now often blurs into the professional territory of the primary school teacher. Inspection and appraisal regimes monitor the teaching/learning processes and compliance with government policies and initiatives; schools and leaders/teachers (and also pupils) that are deemed to be 'failing' are subsequently exposed. School leaders and teachers are accountable to the public with much of their time devoted to activities that arguably relate to accountability rather than leading and/or teaching.

This situation in primary education and the present primary curriculum is rooted in British educational history. Thus, this chapter performs a genealogical analysis illustrating how the curriculum has changed over time and yet has always been a site of conflict because different ideologies or 'traditions' (Blyth, 1965) that dictated curriculum and practice have been emphasized. The more traditionally conservative and classical humanist discourses of education within the primary phase can be 'read' as competing with more liberal-progressive, configuring discourses enshrined in Plowden. The chapter begins by considering the nature of elementary education, which preceded what we now know today as primary education. The analysis examines how, over time, changes in education policy have enabled the shifting of control over curricula content and pedagogy as policy-makers have attempted to address a range of contemporary social, economic and political issues. It is therefore impossible to consider how the primary curriculum has been conceptualized and its nature contested without contemplating and analysing the political, economic, social and historical dimensions in which this change is located. Furthermore, the chapter considers the desire of policy-makers to maintain control over education for the 'masses', the curriculum and regulate the work of elementary/primary teachers. As such, the chapter examines the concurrent erosion of teacher professionalism, resulting in what Campbell (2001) regards as the 'colonisation' of the primary curriculum and the de-professionalization of teachers.

Late nineteenth and early twentieth centuries: The early elementary curriculum and 'payment by results'

In order to comprehend the primary curriculum as it stands in 2012 it is necessary to look back to educational provision some 150 years earlier. The Elementary Education Act of 1870 is the landmark piece of legislation that signalled the beginning of the present state-maintained system of education in Britain; prior to this, public elementary education for the 'labouring poor' was largely provided by the churches (known as voluntary provision). Provision was patchy and concentrated on basic reading, writing and number skills as well as religious instruction. In 1862, the Liberal Government specified the content of the curriculum and divided it into six standards (stages) through 'the Revised Code'[1] (Curtis, 1967). A compulsory syllabus of the rudimentary subjects of reading, writing and arithmetic (commonly known as the 'three Rs') was prescribed for each standard (as well as needlework for girls). The mandated curriculum of the Revised Code fundamentally changed the way teachers worked, how they were remunerated and imposed a strict regime of regulation and supervision. The 'Revised Code' arguably had a number of functions. It concentrated teaching and children's learning on the basic subjects and made more relevant the content of elementary education to the needs of contemporary society rather than merely those of the churches (Richards, 1999). A grant was paid directly to school managers, the amount of which depended on examinations' outcomes in reading, writing and arithmetic, undertaken by external Her Majesty's Inspectorate (HMI) inspectors, and also on pupil attendance. Teachers' salaries were then paid by the school managers and linked to the performance of their pupils. Inspectors were empowered to remove teachers' certificates or 'blacklist' those teachers who failed to meet the required standards (Barber, 1992). Inspectors also monitored the effects of the Code in schools and the extent of schools' compliance with it.

Preparations for the examinations entailed a repetitive and mechanical daily drilling by teachers. Elementary teaching viewed the curriculum as a repository of essential subject matter and skills that teachers transmitted and learning by rote was commonplace (Simon, 1967). Elementary education was essentially concerned with product rather than processes with didactic methods employed so children 'received' the curriculum. Regarding the content of the Code Richards (1999: 55) notes:

> No reference was made to the knowledge, understanding or attitudes to be taught to, or developed within, children; pupils were viewed simply as being able (or unable) to demonstrate a limited number of elementary skills devoid of meaning and context.

Referred to as 'payment by results' this system operated for 35 years in schools and had a marked influence on teaching practice. Although its narrowness was later modified to include other subjects, it was nevertheless successful in 'discouraging initiative and developing habits of obedience, docility and passivity – in teachers as well as in pupils' (Richards, 1999: 55–6). Commenting on the Revised Code at the time as an inspector Kay-Shuttleworth (1868: 143) stated:

> The inspection has been converted into a mechanical examination of these rudiments. The attention of the Managers and Teachers has, by the conditions of the Capitation Grant, been injuriously concentrated on a daily routine of daily drill in reading, writing and ciphering. The result has been a larger amount of failures among the scholars when examined in these subjects, and the general neglect of the higher subjects of instruction, and of cultivation of the general intelligence of the children. The schools are lower in their aims, the scholars worse instructed, and there is a tendency to deterioration in the whole machinery of education.

The imposition of the Revised Code is significant in a number of ways. First, it illustrates the state's desire to exert control over education for the lower classes of the population as well as facilitate social consensus at a time of industrialization, social upheaval and change. While it was believed that some basic literacy, numeracy and religious instruction were potentially beneficial for economic reasons, the shortcomings of the Code ensured that the lower orders would not be 'overeducated' above their station in life, moral docility was maintained and that the existing social stratification was preserved. Eggleston (1977: 32) maintains 'the elementary school emphasised deference, submission and even servility' through low-status subjects and engendering low-status attitudes. Secondly, it demonstrates how elementary teachers themselves were controlled by the state through measures that determined what they taught and how they were paid. When 'payment by results' was withdrawn in 1897, although the government retained oversight of the elementary curriculum, teaching more detailed content was left to the discretion of individual school boards, schools and teachers. However, the constraining conservative practices instilled by 'payment by results' remained for many years; the emphasis on the 3Rs persisted. Other subjects such as geography, history, nature study, gardening (for boys), art and craft, drama, dramatic play and construction activities (for younger children), physical education and music gradually became more commonplace in the elementary classroom from 1897 to 1944 (Richards, 1999).

Pause and ponder

Periodically, the primary curriculum has been criticized for neglecting the 'basics' (i.e. literacy and numeracy). What do you think are the reasons for this criticism and do you think they are justified?

The inter-war years (1918–39): Educational and economic stagnation

Elementary education remained relatively unchanged during the inter-war years which Simon (1991: 25) describes as 'a period of stagnation, both economically and educationally'. Although schools had greater curricular discretion through a less prescriptive and somewhat vague Elementary Code (1926), any change was slow. The publication of the *Handbook of Suggestions for the Consideration of Teachers and Others Concerned in the Work of Elementary Schools* in 1927[2] provided information and guidance to support the Code and the Board of Education's support for teachers to determine their own methods (Richards, 1999). Elementary schools continued to provide education for working class children, but they were largely excluded from secondary education due to its fees, although there was some limited opportunity through places that offered free schooling and scholarships (David, 1980; Tomlinson, 2001). The widening of post-elementary or secondary education was a key aim of the labour movement and Labour Party. Primary and secondary schools date from the Hadow Report of 1926, which reorganized elementary schools into infant schools for 5- to 7-year-olds and junior schools for 7- to 11-year-olds. (Senior schools were for 11- to 14-year-olds). Primary schooling covered children aged 5 to 11 as a whole school, or in two stages (infant and junior). Re-organization along these lines was gradual and slow, however completing in 1972. Streaming of children according to their academic ability was permitted in junior (and senior) schools, regarded at the time as a rational and desirable step and was commonplace by the 1930s (Simon, 1991). While the Hadow Report of 1931 (Board of Education, 1931) acknowledged that primary children required an education suitable to their stage of physical and intellectual development, economic problems impacted upon educational expenditure in the 1930s and no new policies were instigated. David (1980: 59) describes the school system at this time as 'an administrative muddle' and in terms of curricula appraisal and innovation, no such mechanisms existed.

Post-war consensus (1944–70s): The pursuit of equality of opportunity

The post-war era was a period of optimism, reconstruction and potential economic growth. The creation of the welfare state to tackle society's five social 'evils' (want, squalor, idleness, ignorance and disease) was concerned with the 'collective' well-being of individuals and of communities (Williams, 1989). There was general agreement among the political parties of the need for a more interventionist approach by the state (Arnot et al., 1999) and education was perceived as the vehicle through which inequalities and problems in society could be addressed and a new society built (Grace, 1987). In terms of education, the notion of 'equality of opportunity' meant every child was to have educational opportunities regardless of their social class, family background or place of residence (Lowe, 1993; Arnot et al., 1999) and policies were pursued accordingly. The 'Butler' Education Act of 1944 set up a unified system of free, compulsory schooling for children aged 5 to 15 (later 16) and drew a clear distinction between 'primary' and 'secondary' education. The Act represented 'a major step towards the creation of an efficient, cost-effective and 'just' education system' (Lowe, 1993: 198) and a political consensus about the purpose of education in a social democracy ensued. In later years it was apparent that the success/failure of children at 11 years, and which effectively determined children's careers and life chances, was linked to their social background and was effectively reinforcing social differences and reproducing the existing social order (Tomlinson, 2001).

The status of the Board of Education was raised to that of Ministry (later Department of Education and Science, DES) with the authority to 'control and direct LEAs' (Lowe, 1993: 198). After 1944 there was overwhelming support for extra expenditure on education to provide 'opportunity for all'. Between 1950 and 1960 the expenditure on the education system grew faster than any other social service and was the second most expensive, behind social security (Lowe, 1993; Simon, 1991). Demographic changes, the post-war 'baby boom' of mid-1940s and late 1950s, impacted upon schools. Rapid increases in the number of children in primary school, almost one million more in 1954 than in 1944, led to the emergency training of 35,000 extra teachers (Lowe, 1993). The marriage bar was lifted through the 'married women returners' scheme to curtail the shortage of trained teachers as school numbers expanded (Arnot et al., 1999).

Schools were free to determine their own curriculum, which remained under the control of their local authority (the exception was religious instruction, which was centrally prescribed) and the curriculum remained virtually unchanged from the previous period. Primary education post-1944 was dominated however by the requirements of the 11 plus selection examination as the provision of free secondary education for all resulted in the tripartite system comprising grammar, technical and secondary modern schools (Simon, 1991). Children were allocated to one of these schools according to their ability, which was ascertained through the 11 plus examination: narrow, standardized intelligence tests in English and arithmetic. Selection at age 11 meant primary teachers typically prepared older pupils for the 11 plus by coaching, teaching to take tests and practicing tests; this format sometimes trickling back to the education of younger children. Unlike the days of the Revised Code in the late nineteenth century, there was no national assessment system or a rigorous inspection process. Rather, the Ministry of Education commissioned reading surveys and tests periodically for monitoring purposes and HMI played an advisory role to schools (Richards, 1999).

In 1959 the Ministry of Education published *Primary Education: Suggestions for the Consideration of Teachers and Others Concerned with the Work of Primary Schools.* This replaced the previous handbook and took a broader view of what constituted a good education. It also deliberately sought not to be prescriptive but to 'describe the arrangements and practices which are to be found in the more successful schools' (Ministry of Education, 1959: 10: cited in Cunningham; 1988: 15). The handbook reflected a child-centred approach, uniformity of curricular provision, teacher-centred development and teacher autonomy. Cunningham (1988), however, has retrospectively questioned all of this since the content of the handbook dealt mostly with the curriculum rather than child development and, indeed, educational research conducted in the 1970s found little curricular uniformity between schools. Cunningham (1988) suggests other unofficial texts published in the 1940s to 1960s were more influential. He assesses the merits of some of these texts noting how they helped to communicate progressive ideas and principles and thus shape primary teachers' training and practice.

In the 1960s the Labour Government moved 'tentatively towards comprehensive education and curriculum reform' (Tomlinson, 2001: 17). The primary sector had remained neglected until this time when the move to comprehensive education liberated primary schools from the shackles of the 11 plus examination. For the first time in its brief history primary education was seen in its own right as a major stage of educational importance. Simon (1991) illustrates how a small minority of schools had deliberately moved away from streaming pupils and towards a new pedagogic approach in primary teaching with 'informal classrooms' and teachers as facilitators of learning. New ideas to make learning more attractive in primary teaching were experimented with (Spear,

1999). However, it was a major report on primary teaching following a 3-year government-appointed enquiry Plowden (CACE, 1967) that celebrated and endorsed the emerging progressive curriculum and methods and helped to transform primary education and pedagogy.

This particular shift in the curriculum is located in particular in changing societal and economic circumstances of its time. From 1944 onwards changes are evident in lifestyles and living standards, the status of children and the family, popular culture and cultural trends, advances in technology and communications and the role of the mass media. The progressive approach of Plowden placed the individual child at the centre and promoted self-expression, discovery learning with an emphasis on process rather than its products, individual autonomy and choice, personal growth and first-hand experience. This approach inspired many teachers, though not others (Richards, 1999). The enquiry ensured that resources were shifted to the primary sector budget. What followed were extensive building projects, the expansion of teacher training and nursery education. The report advocated greater parental involvement and targeted extra allowances and resources for deprived areas recognized as Educational Priority Areas (David, 1980). Compensatory education and positive discrimination were thus deployed by the Labour Government to combat educational disadvantage (Tomlinson, 2001). The recommendations of Plowden (CACE, 1967) were incorporated into a White[3] Paper (DES, 1972) and a more child-centred approach was adopted in primary education, though many of its intentions were never fully realized because of the changing economic circumstances of 1970s (Wilkinson, 1999). The dominant discourse on primary education as iterated in Plowden (and mooted in the 1931 Hadow Report) was the belief that primary children required an education that was specifically adapted to the stage of their intellectual and physical development. This discourse prevailed until the 1970s.

From 1944 to the mid-1970s teachers enjoyed much freedom over what to teach and a relatively high degree of what Grace (1987: 208) terms 'legitimated professionalism' whereby they established autonomous and effective control of the curriculum. Teachers were seen as having professional knowledge, integrity, expertise and autonomy in the classroom, which he describes as 'the heartland of teacher professionalism' (Grace, 1987: 218). Other than religious education, the

1944 Act had not specified any curricular requirements; teachers thus had control over curricular content and pedagogic methods (Lawton, 1980). They drew on public and political support, expanded their control over curriculum and pedagogy (while working within the frameworks of public examinations and, while it operated, preparing children for the 11 plus) and were responsible for assessment up to the age of 15. Primary teachers were regarded as generalist teachers whose professional expertise was in assisting children's learning. The Schools Council for the Curriculum and Examinations was set up in 1964, an advisory body represented mainly by teachers, and whose very being crystallized a degree of professional autonomy for teachers (Simon, 1991). The relationship between teachers, LEAs and the Ministry of Education (later DES) at this time was one of 'partnership' (Coulby, 1989a). In a discussion of education in the 1960s Simon (1991: 311) observes:

> The curriculum (or what went on in schools) was the specific responsibility of the teachers – not of the local authorities (though their role here was unclear) and certainly not of the state – or the central government. That was an essential factor underlying the functioning of the 'partnership'.

Topic work, which was essentially thematic, cross-curricula and had its roots in progressive education, came to epitomize primary education.

The late 1960s saw changing economic conditions fuelled by declining world economies, which impacted upon funding for education. Despite the massive investment in the post-war years, education was considered expensive while standards remained poor and by 1970s the social-democratic ideology of 'equality of opportunity' was deteriorating. Lowe (1993) however documents a positive improvement on pre-war educational standards at each level after 1944. Reading standards improved considerably and more children were gaining academic qualifications. Nevertheless, there was mounting public concern over education and educational standards. It has been argued that the spectre of falling standards in education 'was being addressed by rhetoric rather than evidence' (Bennett, 1992: 65). However, as Pring (1992) observes, regardless of the 'truth' of these assertions what was more important was the effect of such allegations upon public perceptions of the educational service. The economic crises of the 1970s, rising unemployment and increased international competitiveness fuelled discontent, and in terms of 'value for money' (Lawton, 1980: 11) education was not delivering its promises. The period 1974–80 was characterized by calls for educational reform, greater accountability of the education service and teachers and there was public concern over standards. Attempts were also made to provide empirical, numerical and descriptive data of levels of attainment *actually* reached by pupils and schools (Richards, 1999).

By the mid-1970s equality meant 'equality of outcome' rather than 'equality of opportunity' (Lowe, 1993). In 1974, largely due to concerns about the education of socially disadvantaged and ethnic groups, the Assessment of Performance Unit (APU) was established within the DES with the following brief:

(1) To identify and appraise existing instruments and methods of assessment which may be relevant for these purposes
(2) To sponsor the creation of new instruments and techniques for assessment, having due regard to statistical and sampling methods
(3) To promote the conduct of assessments in co-operation with local education authorities and teachers
(4) To identify significant differences related to the circumstances in which children learn, including the incidence of under-achievement, and to make the findings available to all those concerned with resource allocation within the Department, local authorities and schools. (Chitty, 1989: 79–80)

The establishment of the APU is significant as it marks the first attempt to monitor national standards. However, as David (1980) observes, the unit exceeded its terms of reference and attempted to devise tests of attainment to evaluate the standards of all pupils at different stages of their education. At the same time, a number of LEAs were testing pupils to evaluate school performance in terms of measurable outcomes and others were evaluating teachers' professional performance by gathering descriptive data through more inspections (Richards, 1999). All these developments were partly in response to public and political concern over educational 'standards', originally enunciated by a series of 'Black Papers'[4] (Cox and Dyson, 1969a; 1969b; 1970; Cox and Boyson, 1975; 1977) published by right-wing academics and policy groups. Denouncing politicians, journalists and employers furthered the general disillusionment with education criticizing child-centred, progressive education and advocating a return to traditional teaching methods and disciplines. Linked to the perceived 'crisis' in education was that of the William Tyndale Junior School, Islington, whereby radical progressive methods were utilized against the wishes of parents. This particular 'affair' was captured in sensationalized headlines and marks the beginning of the scrutinizing media coverage of education we are familiar with today (Jones, 2003). Another significant report of this period was the Bullock Report (1975) that investigated the teaching of English and the acquisition and use of the entire range of language skills. It surveyed 2,000 primary schools and the Report, *Language for Life,* made a series of detailed recommendations including, significantly, a system of monitoring. All these various strands outlined above served to fuel general dissatisfaction with education and primary teachers, the standards or levels of competence that should be reached by pupils and schools and these were debated from this period onwards (Richards, 1999).

Jones (2003: 94) purports that by the mid-1970s schooling in England was simultaneously 'radical and conservative'. Schooling was:

> home to curriculum experiment, yet in primary schools, ten years after Plowden, it was still dominated by a traditional pedagogy and a narrow, highly traditional focus on reading and writing . . . It was based on a commitment to equal opportunity yet continued to produce large numbers of unqualified school leavers. (ibid.)

Primary education post-Plowden is often perceived somewhat idealistically and romantically as a 'Golden Age' of teaching and learning and where progressivism was commonplace. Campbell (1993: 216) however explodes the myth contending:

> The curriculum was narrow, emphasising literacy and numeracy through repetitive exercises; despite encouragement, work in science was patchy and haphazard; standards in the social subjects were lower than might be expected; pedagogy was often characterised by an undifferentiated focus in the middle levels of attainment . . . Plowdenesque progressivism flowered largely in rhetoric.

Indeed, educational research (e.g. Alexander, 1984; Galton et al., 1980) and major HMI surveys (DES, 1978; 1982) later revealed a narrow concentration on basic skills and showed the idyllic image of primary schools in the late 1960s and 1970s to be somewhat mythical identifying serious inconsistencies across schools in curriculum breadth, balance, quality and management. As such, an unprecedented speech by Prime Minister James Callaghan at Ruskin College in 1976 sparked what has come to be termed the 'Great Debate' about education (DES, 1977) bringing education into the full arena of public debate and where it has since remained. The 'Ruskin speech' focussed on public concerns about falling standards, pupil dissatisfaction, the economic relevance of education and social failure. Jones (1992: 98) identifies the main issues highlighted in the speech:

> First there was concern over 'methods and aims of informal instruction . . .' Secondly, there was a 'strong case for the so-called core curriculum of basic knowledge'. Thirdly, there was the question of 'monitoring the use of resources in order to maintain a proper national standard of performance'. Fourthly, linked with standards, there was 'the role of the Inspectorate in relation to national standards and their maintenance'. Fifthly, there was 'the need to improve relations between industry and education'. Finally there was the problem of the examination system.

Standards in education became a major issue of government concern (Chitty, 1989) and the Ruskin speech set the agenda for education policy that would ensue in the following years (Williams et al., 1992). Educational and industrial organizations were consulted, as were parents (DES, 1977). Teachers' professional expertise was questioned, they were openly criticized and this reflected a trend towards limiting the boundaries of their autonomy and increasing government intervention in education. The influence of the child-centred approach, though only fully adopted in a minority of primary schools (Simon, 1991), was prevalent and it was argued that progressive teaching failed where inexperienced and less able teachers adopted these informal methods. Whitty (1990: 23) suggests 'trendy teachers' were perceived as 'subverting traditional moral values and selling the nation short'. Secondary schools were criticized because pupils' skills were failing to meet the needs of employers and the requirements of new workplace technologies. A more disciplined structure of learning at all stages in the system was called for along with a 'core curriculum' of basic knowledge and more vocational training (Lowe, 1993). Critics were concerned about the 'secret garden of the curriculum' (Simon, 1991: 448) a term coined by the Conservative Minister of Education, Sir David Eccles. There were calls for the DES to have greater involvement over the shaping of the curriculum, more control over the LEAs and teachers and, more generally, there was growing pressure for accountability. Silver (1990: 2–3) sums up the approach to education from 1960s onwards:

> New emphasis on approaches to the 'world of work' began to influence school curricula and confuse decade-old distinctions between education and training . . . Priorities moved from 'access' to 'excellence' or 'standards', from 'liberal' to more 'vocational' messages.

Indeed, it was becoming apparent that the role of schools was to prepare pupils for the workplace and, due to the unpredictability of society, their learning for life. There are other significant markers that need to be highlighted as these furthered political pressures in the drive for greater consistency and progression in the primary curriculum. First, a study by Bennett (1976) sparked concern and controversy about teaching styles and pupil progress. Secondly the ORACLE project (Galton et al., 1980), which investigated primary practice, drew attention to considerable problems in the curriculum. It also highlighted the lack of whole class interaction, which was connected to the higher cognitive performance by pupils. Thirdly, the HMI survey *Primary Education in England* (DES, 1978), which focused on the junior phase (7–11 years), provided evidence of low expectations of pupil performance by teachers (especially in inner cities), lack of curricula progression, a narrow focus on the basics of English and maths and inadequate and inconsistent provision of other subjects (Campbell, 2003).

Finally there were a number of notable documents (DES, 1981; 1985a) that essentially proposed broad frameworks with the Third Report of the Education Select Committee (House of Commons, 1986) making the case that children should be entitled to common curriculum. This was to be broad, balanced, modern and under the charge of the Secretary of State. The proportion of time then spent per week on English and mathematics equated to approximately 40 per cent, which was far greater than other subjects (approximately 10 per cent each for Physical Education (PE), art, history/geography; approximately

25 per cent for science, technology, music, Religious Education and other teaching) and signified an unbalanced curriculum heavily weighted towards the basics (DES, 1987a). Campbell (2001: 33) describes how 'gentle persuasion delivered a professional consensus about the broad objectives for the primary curriculum' and pupil entitlement. 'Gentle persuasion' for change, however, eventually gave way to political pressures for reform.

1979–97: Conservative policies – centralization and control

The 1988 ERA is another landmark piece of legislation that signalled substantive change (Flude and Hammer, 1990). Between the Ruskin speech and the ERA (as outlined in the previous section) there were growing concerns about the primary curriculum and pedagogy; change was therefore almost inevitable, but the extent of reform was unprecedented. Amongst its many far reaching reforms the ERA empowered the Secretary of State for Education to prescribe a 'balanced and broadly based curriculum' for state-maintained schools. Campbell (2001: 31) conceptualizes this move by government as the 'colonisation of the primary curriculum' whereby, from 1976 onwards, the balance of power shifted away from LEAs, schools and teachers towards central government. Three new bodies were established, the National Curriculum Council (NCC), Curriculum Council for Wales and the School Examinations and Assessment Council (SEAC) (appointed by the Secretary of State) to advise the Secretary of State who made ultimate curricula decisions (Coulby, 1989b). The ERA created greater central control over educational content, changing quite dramatically teachers' ways of working and their professional discretion; however, primary teacher resistance to the National Curriculum was momentary.

The National Curriculum was introduced for all state schools in England and Wales. It incorporated core subjects (English, maths, and science) and foundation subjects (art, geography, history, music, PE and technology; plus a modern foreign language for children over 11 years). Each subject (core and foundation) was to be allocated 'reasonable' time. Curricula commonality and progressive stages, it was proclaimed, would also ensure continuity when children moved schools, rather than having gaps or repetition in their education. While curricula content was specified, its organization, textbooks/materials to be used and particular teaching approaches however were left to teachers' professional discretion although Coulby (1989b: 69) maintains that 'the National Curriculum itself represents a severe restriction on what can be taught in schools'. The highly detailed National Curriculum was phased into primary schools; in 1989 three subjects were introduced into Year 1 and by 1993 all nine subjects were in Years 1 and 4, though the number of subjects varied in the other year groups (2, 3, 5 and 6). Ring-binders for each subject were distributed to schools; these contained Statutory Orders giving teachers information about programmes of study, attainment targets and expected attainments by age level. Topic work which had characterized primary education to some extent was thus potentially threatened. This move towards subject organization in the primary curriculum can be traced back to the HMI primary survey (DES, 1978) where concerns had been raised (Dadds, 1993). Webb (1993: 249) found that teachers in her 1992 study were gradually and regretfully moving away from 'broad-based topics to subject-focused topics' in order to 'achieve National Curriculum coverage and facilitate the assessment and recording of attainment'. To reflect this initial teacher training changed to focus on the production of subject specialists (instead of the generalist primary teacher) with the emphasis on teaching rather than pupil learning.

The ERA established a mandatory national system of pupil assessment, in the form of SATs. In primary schools children aged seven (Key Stage One, Year 2) and 11 (Key Stage Two, Year 6) were examined in the core subjects. Children were assessed against the expected 'standard' for their age so children age seven would be expected to achieve Level 2 and children age 11, Level 4. Brown and Lauder (1992: 23) suggest:

> The notion of standards has come to be defined in terms of standardisation: the selection and packaging of knowledge into discreet subject areas, the labelling of students with an IQ score, and badges of ability gained by amassing qualifications.

While purported to merely provide 'objective' indicators of quality, in practice they have provided crude and often misleading data with no attempt to allow for different levels of funding or the social composition of pupils (Gillborn and Youdell, 2000). The league tables encourage schools to compete by exposure to market forces and performance indicators of this kind have become central to evaluating performance in schools. The new assessment procedures ensured that educational outcomes or 'standards' of different age groups could be measured across schools providing comparative information and ensuring schools' accountability (Butterfield, 1995). Adaptations to the curriculum and testing in the late 1980s and early 1990s led to a 'deluge of directives' from the government (Webb and Vulliamy, 1996) to clarify and extend the ERA, with 'non-statutory' advice from the NCC and SEAC to accompany the ring-binders. Whereas up to the ERA there had been some reluctance by policy-makers to determine methods or the 'how' of teaching in schools, increasingly however, the then Secretary of State for Education, Kenneth Clarke, intervened both in the content and pedagogy of the primary curriculum attacking child-centred education as thwarting effective delivery. As such, a review was commissioned resulting in the publication of a document *Curriculum Organisation and Classroom Practice in Primary Schools* (Alexander et al., 1992). This document, alternatively known as the Three Wise Men Report, focussed on the nature and quality of primary pedagogy, reviewing evidence and making recommendations. The Dearing Review (Dearing, 1993), also commissioned by the Secretary of State, was designed to slim down the curriculum. For example, it proposed 'discretionary time' the rhetoric of which freed schools from the shackles of prescription for the equivalent of a day a week, although in reality this was not possible (Campbell, 2003).

New forms of school inspection emerged in 1992 through the establishment of OfSTED, which replaced HMI. OfSTED monitors activities in schools and ensures the proper delivery of the curriculum. Arguably, this new form of external surveillance and control was to ensure that schools were complying with the government's agenda. OfSTED initially published inspection reports on every school every 4 years, which has led to public 'naming and shaming' of schools. 'Failing schools', those failing to meet required standards and sitting towards the bottom of league tables, are thus more easily identified.

Leading up to the change of government in 1997 there are a number of significant developments that can be determined from the post-1979 period of Conservative Governments. Any curricula experimentation by teachers was not allowed after 1989; the ERA coupled with the 'imposition' of a National Curriculum effectively terminated the relative freedom enjoyed by teachers in the post-war era. The notion of teachers as independent, autonomous professionals, which had been established in the preceding decades when they had expanded the curriculum, demanding greater resources and monopolized provision (Ozga, 1995) was completely eroded. As had begun in the mid-1970s, 'ineffective teachers' were blamed throughout the 1980s for the decline in British industry and commerce and the high numbers of young unemployed who lacked sufficient skills and knowledge (Coulby, 1989a). This populist position fed parental and public concern and was perpetuated by a concerted press campaign. Central control of education under the Conservatives was tightened, although the actual impact of the National Curriculum in primary schools at this time remains unclear. Some studies reported change along the lines of government policies (e.g. the Bristol 'PACE' project, Pollard et al., 1994); others however indicate continuity with previous practice (Alexander, 1997; Campbell and Neill, 1994). What is certain is that on the eve of the 1997 general election there was renewed impetus for change; the anticipation and expectation was that a Labour Government would be different.

Over to you . . .

Now read the chapter by Jim Campbell

See: Campbell, R.J. (2001) 'The colonisation of the primary curriculum', in R. Phillips and J. Furlong (eds) *Education Reform and the State: Twenty-five Years of Politics, Policy and Practice*, London: RoutledgeFalmer.

Campbell discusses what he terms the 'colonisation of the primary curriculum'.

(1) What do you think he means by this?

(2) In your opinion, is his view justified?

1997–2010: New Labour policies – tighter governmental control

In the closing decades of the twentieth century the restructuring of world economies and the introduction of new technologies simultaneously created greater political uncertainties and demanded highly skilled, flexible and differentiated labour forces to secure future economic success. Governments in countries around the globe were aligning the aims of their respective education systems with the perceived needs of their country's industry and economy. As such, education policy was given a very high profile in the United Kingdom under the New Labour Government of 1997. The expectation of many was that far reaching changes would be made in the education sector by the incoming government. New Labour's early educational reforms however largely consolidated those of the previous Conservative administration. Policy reversals were notably the abolition of the Nursery Voucher and Grant-maintained Schools and phasing out the Assisted Places Scheme. Otherwise, almost all the other reforms and measures introduced by the Conservatives continued in place. Perhaps the most notable difference was the reluctance by New Labour to rely merely on market forces to raise standards in schools, and to intervene more directly in education. While there was greater delegation of powers to schools, there was simultaneously increased centralization through the meeting of nationally set targets. While the publicly stated objective of the Conservative's ERA had been to 'raise standards' in schools expectations appeared to have fallen somewhat short. When international comparisons were made with other industrialized countries (particularly those in South East Asia), standards in schools in England (and Wales) were not rising fast enough (DfEE, 1997a: 78–84) and the achievement of pupils in terms of human capital formation was presented as 'just not good enough' (DfEE, 1997a: 10, para. 9). Further government intervention, it was purported, was thus warranted in the processes of schooling and the control of teachers' work to ensure that the government's ultimate aspirations of 'raising standards' in schools were to be met and what New Labour described as a 'world-class education service' was achieved. While education was given more prominence for economical purposes those charged with the responsibilities of producing the workforce, namely teachers, were publicly criticized with scathing attacks on the profession from policy-makers (Rafferty and Barnard, 1998; Webster and O'Leary, 1999).

During its first term in office (1997–2001) primary schools were targeted by New Labour as a site for modernization (DfEE, 1998a). 'New' extra funding came into the education service and the neglect by policy-makers that the primary phase had endured over the previous 25 years or so ended. 'Modernization' of the primary curriculum entailed greater flexibility for teachers, but a more prescriptive primary pedagogy with the introduction of the centrally determined primary strategies. The work of the Literacy Task Force, set up initially by the Labour Party in 1996, coming to fruition in the Literacy Strategy and the National Numeracy Task Force was established in 1998 by Secretary of State, David Blunkett. In the pursuit of raising standards in primary schools the government intervened directly with the introduction of the Literacy Hour (DfEE, 1998b) and Numeracy Scheme (DfEE, 1998c), which detailed content and methods for the daily teaching of literacy and numeracy. Government targets for Key Stage Two required that 80 per cent of pupils reached the expected standard for their age (Level 4) in literacy by 2002 (attainment was 63 per cent in 1997) and 75 per cent reached the expected standard for their age (Level 4) in numeracy (attainment was 62 per cent in 1997) (Docking, 2000). Blunkett's promise in May 1997 to resign from his post as Secretary of State for Education and Employment if these targets were not met in 2002 caused problems for the then current Secretary of State, Estelle Morris, when the results fell short. In 2002 attainment in literacy was 75 per cent and 73 per cent for numeracy (Smithers, 2002). While politically the numeracy and literacy targets may be important indicators for policy-makers, in the short term they represent a somewhat narrow definition of primary education. This level of intervention and prescription was, arguably, far from modern and harked back to the nineteenth century system of the Elementary School Code. Teaching materials and training were developed for teachers while the revised programme for trainee teachers focused on the standards and strategies. Teachers' work intensified (Forrester, 2000), which resulted for some as stress and burnout because of the pressure to maximize pupil outcomes. The message from New

Labour was evident however; teachers could not be trusted in realizing the world-class education system the government envisaged or implement the top down, standards agenda; intervention and prescription were therefore deemed necessary and were enforced by OfSTED. Furthermore, the Chief Inspector of Schools at OfSTED, Chris Woodhead, was a known traditionalist with an aversion to progressive education (see Woodhead, 2002). Without a doubt, New Labour's ideological approach shifted the primary curriculum further away from child-centredness.

The National Curriculum underwent a review in 1997; the outcome was more prominence being given to literacy and numeracy to enable schools to meet the 2002 targets. This was to be at the expense of subjects such as music, art and PE, which were squeezed, and hence distorted the 'balanced' curriculum. Primary teaching became more 'test orientated' as league table performance reflected Key Stage Two test scores. Teachers' pay became linked to their performance in 2000 (Forrester, 2005) and teachers inevitably were tempted to teach more to test requirements. Again, there is some resonance here with the nineteenth century system, payment by results. It was apparent by 2000 to policy-makers that improvements in SATs had probably reached a plateau and continual improvement was impossible due to the constraints of social structures beyond the school gates (i.e. communities with high deprivation, low aspirations). An evaluation of the strategies by OfSTED (2005) found that improvements in literacy and numeracy teaching were substantial though identified weaknesses associated with poor management of the strategies in schools. Another significant review (Earl et al., 2003) found while there was more whole class teaching (i.e. teacher-centred pedagogy) the effect of the strategies on pupil learning was less clear. The realization that target setting was failing in the standards agenda was coupled with pressure from elsewhere; the think-tank Demos, for example, expressed concerns about the mismatch between the curriculum and the needs of a global economy and post-industrialism where innovation and creativity are vital for business success. Also, other high performing Asian economies such as Singapore were giving greater prominence to creativity, problem-solving and project work in the school curriculum (Tan and Gopinathan, 2000). Creativity, greater autonomy for teachers, less prescription and fewer targets were subsequently advocated in the new primary strategy *Excellence and Enjoyment* (DfES, 2003a) as was an individualized form of learning conceptualized as 'personalised learning' deemed vital for the 'knowledge economy' (Hartley, 2003). It is interesting to note, however, that while New Labour's view of person-alized learning was presented as 'not a return to child-centred theories' (Miliband, 2006: 24), the five components of personalized learning identified, such as 'accommodating different paces and styles of learning' (ibid.: 24) and 'every student enjoying curriculum choice, a breadth of study and personal relevance' (ibid.: 25) do correspond very closely to the tenants of progressive, child-centeredness. Thus, this once again provides evidence of the inherent tensions that operate within the curriculum.

The most extensive, comprehensive enquiry of primary education since Plowden, the Cambridge Primary Review, was undertaken between 2006 and 2009 by a team of academics and professionals led by Professor Robin Alexander. This was a major independent review, funded by the charity Esmée Fairbairn Foundation, and enquired into the 'condition and future of primary education'. The Review generated a phenomenal mix of evidence from thousands of written submissions, surveys of existing research and soundings held in different locations. It produced many interim reports and briefing papers; there were numerous regional dissemination conferences, media articles and a substantial final report comprising 24 chapters, 78 formal conclusions and 75 recommendations for policy and practice (Alexander, 2009). The reviewers condemned what they regarded as a 'state theory of learning'. While the Review generated extensive media coverage, some of the findings were hijacked along the way and presented, by the tabloid press especially, in a sensationalist and scaremongering manner. Such reporting inevitably impacted negatively upon the already uneasy relationship between the Review team and the government as Ministers were obliged to respond to the media hype that hurled criticism at 'failed' government initiatives (Alexander, 2010). Given the extent and breadth of this Review, it is very difficult to summarize its research, analysis, conclusions and recommendations in this space. Notably, however, and in relation to some of the issues raised in this chapter, the Final Report concludes that the emphasis on tests, targets and prescriptive methods has probably contributed to depressed standards overall by constricting teachers, thwarting their creativity and diminishing their ability to teach. The Report purports:

> Children will not learn to think for themselves if their teachers are expected merely to do as they are told. (Alexander, 2009: 496)

The Review had a broad remit of ten educational themes. The Interim Report by Wyse et al. (2008) which reviewed published research for the third theme illuminates some of the complexities surrounding the primary curriculum and assessment. Solutions to the current 'problems' in primary schools include extending the foundation stage to age six, developing a curriculum that comprises eight domains of knowledge and targeting pupils who are deprived. The Review's dedicated website[5] is also a repository for a wealth of information. Whether the UK Government will eventually take on board the totality of this Review remains to be seen; the New Labour Government was hesitant, the Coalition Government seems to be more receptive. However, what the Review has done is opened up the debate about primary education in the public domain and unquestionably raised the profile of primary education.

The Cambridge Review also challenged the Rose Review, which was New Labour's own 'independent' review of the primary curriculum commissioned in 2008. The outcome of this review, the Rose Review (2009), was the proposal of six areas of learning that combined the traditional subjects: understanding English, communication and languages; mathematical understanding; scientific and technological understanding; historical, geographical and social understanding; understanding physical development, health and well-being and understanding the arts. This new curriculum was due to be implemented in schools in September 2011; however, it was subsequently shelved by the incoming Coalition Government following the general election in the United Kingdom in May.

2010 onwards: Coalition policies – more change, or more of the same?

The document *The Coalition: Our Programme for Government* (Cabinet Office, 2010) was published almost immediately after the coalition took up office and set out the priorities for the Coalition Government in Westminster. The section on 'Schools' which comprised 17 bullet points gave the first indication of the new government's educational agenda. Two of these have particular relevance to this chapter:

- We will promote the reform of schools in order to ensure that new providers can enter the state school system in response to parental demand; that all schools have greater freedom over the curriculum; and that all schools are held properly to account. (ibid.: 28)
- We will keep external assessment, but will review how Key Stage 2 tests operate in future. (ibid.: 29)

Subsequent developments saw a call for a review of the National Curriculum in January 2011 and at the time of writing Tim Oates of the University of Cambridge was chairing the panel of experts overseeing the curriculum review with the 3-month 'call for evidence' generating over 2,200 responses. The review is deemed as 'open and outward-facing' (DfE, 2011b); the outcome is currently unknown although early indications from the DfE suggest that:

> the new National Curriculum will set out only the essential knowledge that all children should acquire, and give schools and teachers more freedom to decide how to teach this most effectively and to design a wider school curriculum that best meets the needs of their pupils. (ibid.)

The DfE's Review timetable indicates a public consultation in 2012 and new programmes being made available to schools and being rolled out by September 2014. While the outcome remains uncertain, what is evident is that the primary curriculum is likely to experience remarkable change.

Pause and ponder

Primary education encapsulates a range of different competing traditions, ideologies and educational philosophies that have permeated its culture at different historical moments and continue to do so. In your opinion, are these complementary or contradictory?

What do you consider are the main surviving legacies and reoccurring themes in the evolving primary curriculum?

Notes

1 The Elementary Code comprised the curriculum and prescribed nationally what (elementary) teachers taught in their schools.
2 *Suggestions for the Consideration of Teachers and Others Concerned in the Work of Elementary Schools,* written primarily by HM Inspectors, was first published by the Board of Education in 1905 following the Code of 1904. It showed 'effective' teaching though shaped opinion and policy rather than practice. A subsequent edition (1937) and reprint (1942) changed little.
3 White Papers are a declaration of government policy (Command Papers).
4 The term 'Black Paper' intentionally signals a contrast with Government White Papers.
5 www.primaryreview.org.uk

Further reading

Alexander, R.J. (ed.) (2009) *Children, Their World, Their Education: Final Report and Recommendations of the Cambridge Primary Review,* Abingdon: Routledge.
Campbell, R.J. (2001) 'The colonisation of the primary curriculum', in R. Phillips and J. Furlong (eds) *Education Reform and the State. Twenty-Five Years of Politics, Policy and Practice,* London: RoutledgeFalmer.
Richards, C. (1999) *Primary Education – At a Hinge of History?* London: Falmer Press.

5 Post-compulsory Education

Introduction

The relationship between education and the economy has a long and chequered history dating back to the late nineteenth century. Yet such well known links have been described at best 'tenuous' (Young, 1993) or worse, 'mythical' (Wolf, 2002). It would be remiss *not* to point out then that the politics of education policy is influenced by a broad range of social, cultural and historical factors, as well as important economic ones, as we have sought to demonstrate throughout this book. Here, we suggest the apparent link between education and training and the modern economy is apt to reflect the nuances of particular social, cultural and political milieu: the enduring histories and traditions of industrial economies and their respective nation states (Green, 1990). In this chapter we focus on the influence of the late-capitalist economy upon the landscape of post-compulsory education and training in England, and consider why even today this mysterious relationship continues to dominate the hearts and minds of politicians, policy-advisors, educationalists and critical commentators alike. More especially and fundamentally, we suggest there remains a pathological belief in the ability of education to provide a panacea for the perceived ills of the economy and contemporary society. As David Cameron, leader of the Coalition Government recently proclaimed:

> For youth unemployment, which has actually been going up for years in our country, the real change we need is actually in our education system to make sure we are producing young people at the age of 18 with a *real qualification* that people need in the modern workplace. (Cameron quoted in *The Telegraph*, 2011: emphasis added)

Here the term 'real qualification' is revealing, but perhaps more for what it does *not* say than what it appears to assert. The ambition to produce young people with 'real qualifications' posits an 'authentic ideal' in the future against the perceived 'inauthentic' system of the present, where an argument for 'real change' is made. Further, by implying that contemporary education is in some way 'lacking', its maligned status is affirmed and, with this, the notion of the 'inauthentic' to produce inferior qualifications is effectively reinforced, where credentials (including degrees) are reported as being not 'worth the paper they're printed on' (Walker E. 2008). This argument forms a recurring theme throughout the chapter, as the notion of what counts as relevant and real in educational terms has tended to become conflated with the changing preferences of modern politicians, while evolving alongside more radical, structural change in the political economy; change that continues, to this day, to be influenced by the hegemony of neo-liberal ideology. For now though, it is perhaps worth contemplating how such an idea was initially conceived, and to consider why the apparent link between post-compulsory education and the economy is perceived so remarkably precious to the future prosperity of our society?

The birth of instrumentalism: The academic and vocational divide

In the aftermath of the industrial revolution, modern industrial economies increasingly relied upon a separation of 'mental' and 'manual' labour as a means to justify a similar partition of academic and vocational education and training (Young, 1993). Underlying such historical divisions in the provision of formal education was a popular belief in the ability of school-based education or work-based training to provide the engine for economic growth (Wolf, 2002). This became increasingly apparent as the nature and role of the economy changed over time and with this too, its relationship with post-compulsory education. During the last decades of the nineteenth century and throughout the early–mid twentieth century, mass production paved the way for increasing levels of specialization at work, levels which relied, in turn, on a more clearly defined and extensive division of labour – between the creative conception of tasks and their simple execution and production (Piore and Sabel, 1984). Such divisive specialization, upon which the political economy of mass-production depended, made it necessary that waged labour possesses no more than the most rudimentary education and work-related skills, just sufficient, in fact, to enable the routine and timely production of goods and services. In this crucial respect it was the inertia of the capitalist economy that produced severe constraints upon the growth of formal (academic) education, where a separation of 'minds' was created (and acknowledged much later in the Crowther Report [MoE, 1959]), producing an instrumental rationale for the development of selective education: an early-selection, low participation system (Finegold et al., 1990: 14).

Activity

Trawl the national newspapers and find as many articles as possible featuring the virtues of academic education, and then do the same for vocational education. Using the cuttings as evidence, develop an argument both for and against the promotion of a divided system of education: academic and vocational.

Changing times, changing conditions

During the mid-late twentieth century a radical transformation and restructuring of the nature and state of the political economy began to emerge. As patterns of trade changed, through increasing globalization (see Chapter 7), there was a marked 'shift away from the closed or walled economies of the post-war period towards an open or global economy', where 'national "champions" such as Ford, IBM, ICI and Mercedes Benz ... tried to break free of their national roots, creating a *global auction* for investment, technology and jobs' (Brown and Lauder, 1996: 2: original emphasis). This produced a significant departure from the earlier reliance on mass production (or *Fordism*, so named after Henry Ford who created a low-cost and standardized process of manufacture) and divisive specialization, as capital became more mobile, enabling the process and techniques of mass production to be relocated in countries and regions offering 'low wage costs, light labour market legislation, weak trade unions ... and cheap rent' (ibid.: 2). Fundamental change in the international economy coupled with increasing competition from external foreign markets meant that many traditional heavy industries fell into permanent inexorable decline. The post-war boom had ended and mass production was proving so uncompetitive as to be gradually replaced by a burgeoning service and technology-inspired sector, demanding new 'human-capital', knowledge, skills and 'entrepreneurial acumen in an unfettered global marketplace' (ibid.: 3).

Thus, whereas previously the internal resistance of a more domestically contained political economy had helped determine the purpose and selective function of education, the new global order was beginning to privilege the concept of flexible specialization, especially at the turn of the twenty-first century. More than ever, this meant there was now a requirement for workers to become more adaptable and responsive to change in the so-called 'global auction' (Brown and Lauder, 1996). A continuous demand for new knowledge and skills was created along with the possibility of several changes in employment over the course of a lifetime. As Young (1993: 208: original emphasis) suggests, such a conception of political economy 'depends on prior education and political changes . . . [in] an era of education (or more broadly human resource-led) economic growth', and where '*national systems of education and training, rather than national economies* . . . will determine the fate of nations'. This suggests that while the union between education and the modern economy became more strongly wedded, the quality of this marriage changed substantially over time. Both formal schooling and contemporary post-compulsory education became a prior condition in the move to serve the needs of the economy and a new global order.

Economic and political context

The 1970s marked a watershed in the rise of the political New Right (see Chapter 1) and its revolutionary impact on education and the economy. At the end of the 1960s, the post-war, welfare-capitalist consensus that had held sway since the end of the Second World War finally began to recoil. The oil crisis of the early 1970s represented the start of a steep decline throughout the decade matched with unprecedented social, political and economic transformation and restructuring (Jones, 2003; Brown and Lauder, 1996), signalling the end of the so-called golden age. 'Mounting inflation, swelling balance of payments deficits, unprecedented currency depreciation, rising unemployment [especially youth unemployment (Finegold et al., 1990)], and bitter industrial conflicts' (Marquand, 1988: 3, cited in Chitty, 2009: 32) all served to reinforce the feeling that Keynesian social democracy had failed and had had its day, and that radical economic and political change was now urgently needed (see also Chapter 6).

Emerging in tandem with the economic crisis of the period was the widely perceived calamity of state education. As noted in Chapters 1 and 4, the *Black Papers,* written by right-wing dissenting educationalists and politicians, were influential in portraying the idea that state education had descended into chaos, and that such profound destabilization was especially worrying in the context of unprecedented global economic decline. Such events proved significant as a catalyst in synthesizing several strands of thought, and in further establishing a platform for the launch of James Callaghan's (then Labour prime minister) Ruskin College Speech, at Oxford in 1976 (Phillips and Furlong, 2001). The speech, and well-publicized call for a 'Great Debate' on education that followed, centred upon two major areas of concern: 'standards and behaviour in schools, and the supply of skilled manpower, especially scientists, engineers and technologists' (Moore, 1984: 72). As Callaghan (1976) argued at the time:

> I have been very impressed in the schools I have visited . . . But I am concerned on my journeys to find complaints from industry that new

recruits from the schools sometimes do not have the basic tools to do the job that is required . . . There seems to be a need for more technological bias in science teaching that will lead towards practical applications in industry rather than towards academic studies . . . To what extent are these deficiencies the result of insufficient co-operation between schools and industry? . . . There is the need to improve relations between industry and education.

The impact of Callaghan's prime ministerial intervention reverberated throughout the education world and gave political sanction to the so-called '"discourse of derision" mounted by the *Black Papers*', as well as further impetus to an 'increasingly well-organised and articulate New Right' (Ball, 1990: 31–2). As Tomlinson (2008b: 25) explains: 'wide publicity was given to employers and business people who argued that comprehensive schools did not serve the needs of British industry, and from this time educational practices were to become more closely linked to industrial regeneration'. More than ever before, the nature and purpose of education came to be seen as a central plank of political thinking, and thus crucially implicated in the construction of other social and economic realities, in particular the view that education and training post-16 was 'failing to meet the needs of an advanced industrial economy' (Finegold, 1993: 42). In effect, Callaghan's speech served to galvanize the link between education and the economy, and further provided the logic of justification for a more directive approach to post-compulsory education and training in the context of a radically changing economy.

The New Right: Market reforms and post-compulsory education

The impact of the Ruskin speech, mobilizing a series of debates and government-inspired policy texts (e.g. DES, 1977; DE/DES, 1986), gave credence to a 'new vocationalism' at the beginning of the 1980s, forging strong links between education and industry. For the New Right, a key point of departure involved challenging the long-stranding, anti-industrial culture in Britain, by attempting to instil the 'right' sort of attitudes in young people towards business, industry and the workplace. This entailed challenging the perceived neglect of basic (work-related) skills in education (see, for example, *A Basis for Choice* [FEU, 1979]), as well as encouraging an understanding in young people about the world of work and industry, and its important role in wealth creation for the benefit of society and the economy. Refocusing teachers' and schools' attention on the value of the 'practical and vocational' alongside the 'academic' signalled the beginning of a broad shift, for the right-wing Conservative Government (1979–97) was intent on fostering a spirit of enterprise and entrepreneurship through all sectors of education (Ball, 1990). Some of these concerns were addressed through innovation and change in educational provision, for example, through the introduction of the Technical and Vocational Education Initiative (TVEI) (intended to relate education to the world of work for 14–18 year olds). However, TVEI did not reform the certification system, nor did it 'address broader issues arising either from the division between academic and vocational studies or from the institutional break at 16' (Finegold et al., 1990: 12). Indeed, at the time TVEI was introduced (along with a raft of other vocational programmes intended to make education more relevant to the economy), the late Sir Keith Joseph, Secretary of State for Education (1981–86) declared that such pathways were only properly intended for the 'bottom 40 per cent' of achievers (Rowan, 1997).

A key feature of the political New Right was its fundamental faith in the 'market analogue' (Finegold, 1993) – a system sensitive to considerations of efficiency, cost-effectiveness and notions of individual learner flexibility. For perhaps the first time during the 1980s, the discipline of the market, a corrective to excessive interference of public agencies in the economy, entered the process of education and training creating a paradigm shift (Hodkinson and Sparkes, 1995). This meant that rather than state bureaucracies taking decisions on important matters of contemporary education and training, individual market freedom would prevail, with 'choice' being given over to students rebranded as 'consumers' of education. However, the emphasis on the individual was double-edged invoking elements of freedom *and* coercion. For example, in a government White Paper (see Chapter 1 for a definition of White Paper), *Working Together – Education and Training* (DE/DES, 1986: 1.4), this tension emerged through the role of the individual reconceived as autonomous learner, where it was argued that in the process of learning: 'motivation is all important so that attitudes change and people acquire the desire to learn, the habit of learning, and the skills learning brings'. This perspective is especially significant for it implies that at the root of the economic problem lies something of a benign pathology: the attitudes, skills and abilities of the *individual,* whereas Stronach (1988: 60) suggests, 'the personalising of economic competitiveness (be motivated, get skilled) offers both an economics of recovery and a metonymics of blame (if *you* were trained and motivated *we* wouldn't be where we are today)' (cited in Ball, 1990: 74).

In 1988 a different White Paper, *Training for Employment*, pointed to 'the changing circumstances of the youth labour market' (DE, 1988: 6.12), from which the then Training Agency announced the introduction of a new model of Youth Training. In this the government phased out 'paying an allowance for trainees under the rationale that in increasingly tight labour markets employers would be competing to take on young people' (Finegold, 1993: 46). To this end, in 1990 an 'individual training credit' or voucher programme was piloted, in which *individuals* would become, once again, 'more demanding consumers of training while encouraging competition among the providers by giving 16 year olds a credit to cover the costs of training up to at least NVQ level II' (ibid.: 46). This move was perfectly aligned with the new culture of market reforms based on the binary of choice and blame, noted above. After all, with a scheme of individual credits young people 'have consciously to choose *not* to enhance their skills' (ibid.: emphasis added) – that is consciously opt-out of learning. Underpinning this was the Confederation of British Industry's (CBI) notion of careership in which 'pride of place' was given 'to the individual and his or her responsibility for self-development in a market environment' (1993: 13). Accordingly, any absence of interest and motivation on the part of the learner could be attributed directly to a personal deficit. As the CBI noted 'relevant qualifications and trans-ferable core skills [are] needed by employers and employees alike' (ibid.), where the role of the individual in managing his/her own learning can be regarded as an important 'process skill' (CBI, 1989; 1993) (of which, more later).

A third White Paper, *Education and Training for the 21ˢᵗ Century* (DfE/ED/WO, 1991), brought yet further significant change to the landscape of post-compulsory education, at a time of wider societal and economic instability at the start of the 1990s (Hodgson and Spours, 1997). A steady rise in full-time participation post-16 in the late 1980s and into the following decade shifted the balancing point from a traditional equilibrium of 'low participation' to one of 'medium participation' (Spours, 1995). Meanwhile the government persisted with characteristic zeal in its ideological mission to improve 'supply-side' conditions, enabling the market to function more flexibly and efficiently and emphasizing 'the power and autonomy of individual students and individual institutions' (Hodgson and Spours, 1997: 9). This was achieved through the introduction of the 1992 Further and Higher Education Act, which secured a 'quasi-market' (Levacic, 1995) in post-compulsory education. The strategic removal of sixth-form, tertiary and further education colleges from local authority control was initiated in a bid to increase efficiency and drive up quality (Hodgson and Spours, 2006). At the same time, control of the state's finances for training were strategically transferred 'to a group of new, local employer-led Training and Enterprise Councils (TECs) . . . to mobilise local employers to play a greater role' (Finegold, 1993: 47). Unfortunately, the latter coincided with a weakening of the youth labour market exacerbated by the onset of economic recession in the early 1990s. This led ironically to a situation in which employers 'hunkered' down, and so the tradition of cutting training during times of financial stringency continued, for fear of a situation in which expensively trained workers might 'be poached' (Hodkinson and Sparkes, 1995: 190).

In this changing environment, the White Paper of 1991 sought to provide a more centralized approach to qualifications reform, principally through the formalization of a triple-track: academic (A-levels), vocational (GNVQs) and occupationally specific (NVQs) (Hodgson and Spours, 1997). This came against a backdrop of discussion to develop a unified system of qualifications, comprising both general (academic) and vocational education culminating in a *British Baccalaureate* (Finegold et al., 1990). The economic rationale was in tune with the feeling that A-levels alone were unable to provide 'particular capacities' and 'skills' for the workplace (this had long been the CBI's argument) (Young, 1997). In recognition of this fact, just three years earlier the Higginson Report (DES, 1988) had advised on the reform of A-levels, suggesting that they needed to be leaner, broader and less specialized to meet the twin demands of rising participation and flexible specialization, an important prerequisite of future economic success. Despite this fact, the 1991 White Paper served to retrench them, by restricting access and participation through modified assessment (making them 'tougher') and developing a clear vocational alternative through the introduction of GNVQs (Hodgson and Spours, 1997). Moreover, as participation rates grew from 50 per cent to about 70 per cent between 1987 and 1994, the government further exercised its neo-conservative arm of 'social authoritarianism' (Johnson and Steinberg, 2004). The introduction of more structure and centralization through National Training Targets for Education and Training (originating from the CBI) and a new National Vocational Qualifications framework served to enhance the 'market analogue' as a basis to drive up standards. Thus, much like the National Curriculum had usefully created a centralized system of standardization (of curricula and assessment), to facilitate comparison between schools in a competitive market environment, so competence-related NVQs would serve a similar purpose and allow the state to play 'a less interventionist role' (Finegold, 1993: 48) in the market, while simultaneously catering to the 'job-related training needs' (Spours, 1997: 57) and demands of employers. Throughout, the focus on the responsibility of the individual would be paramount, as a 1994 White Paper, *Competitiveness: Helping Business Win,* indicated: 'a fulfilled workforce meeting *individual targets,* driven by the will to perform to their *individual best,* will be a world class workforce' (Government White Paper, 1994: 30).

At the end of the Conservative Government's (1979–97) political reign came the publication of the Dearing Report on 16–19 qualifications (Dearing, 1996a). Like many policy texts, both before and since, the Report conveyed an ambiguous message to the debate on post-16 reform, and perhaps deliberately so in order to satisfy a broad range of 'educational and political constituencies' (Young, 1997: 25). Essentially, the Report pointed towards the development of a more unified system of qualifications and their consolidation, more emphasis on 'core skills' (albeit only for those involved with GNVQs), and the need to achieve greater parity of esteem between academic and vocational pathways. This coincided with growing recognition of increasing levels of participation, along with a desire to minimize the wastage of talent (as A-levels were reaching only one in three people [Young and Leney, 1997]), and further enhance competitiveness through improved qualifications for the whole population (DTI, 1995). However, despite the call to an overarching framework for an Advanced Diploma, bringing different qualifications together (including A-levels), the reality was that many right-wing politicians remained suspicious of change, especially when such radical reform posed a threat to the selective function of A-levels, and, with this, the view that only a 'very small number of students could possibly do well at [them]' (Young and Leney, 1997: 48). As such, notions of breadth and flexibility, articulated as part of the modernizing agenda – (a rhetoric to develop a high-participation, high-skill and high-wage economy), appear at odds with the divisive function of A-levels, and, correspondingly, the enduring elitist belief that enhanced participation must equate with a decline in academic standards. Indeed, the Advanced Diploma was not so much posed as a replacement for A-levels, in the way the *Baccalaureate* had been (Finegold et al., 1990), but rather as a 'weak-framework' designed to capture existing qualifications, while at the same time preserving different forms of assessment (as opposed to unitizing them) and reinforcing the value of 'core-skills' (later proposed as a qualification in 'key-skills' to link the different qualification tracks [Dearing cited in DfEE, 1997c]). In retrospect the Dearing Report (1996a) can be viewed as a reincarnation of the 1991 White Paper, which dates back to the spirit of Crowther (MoE, 1959), and before that the long history of academic/vocational divisions noted at the beginning of the chapter. Looking forward, maybe this is what David Cameron means by 'real qualifications' and a changed education system: a return in the future to good old-fashioned elitism?

New Labour: But more of the same?

The radical reconfiguration of post-compulsory education and training along economic lines during the 1980s and 1990s created a competitive, marketized system in which educational services were rebranded as 'commodities' and sold to student-consumers in the marketplace. This transformation heralded the beginning of a new mixed economy of private and public-sector institutions competing for education business in an environment in which notions of educational welfare were effectively displaced by a new *modus operandi* in which only the fittest survived (see Chapter 6). Yet while the market economy promised much in the way of addressing the inflexibilities associated with the above-mentioned Fordist model of divisive specialization in a low-skill economy – (by increasing participation and driving up standards), paradoxically the New Right's market reforms served only to colonize academic education and thus:

> school the majority of children for a neo-Fordist economy which requires a low level of talent and skill . . . in the context of the global auction, the market reforms are likely to leave a large majority of the future working population without the human resources to flourish in the global economy. (Brown and Lauder, 1996: 7–8)

It is against this backdrop that New Labour's approach (1997–2010) to post-compulsory education and training, across three terms of office, signalled both points of continuity and change in relation to previous Conservative education policy. Much like their predecessors, New Labour was similarly committed to achieving higher standards in education and thus establishing 'greater relevance to economic performance' (Pring, 2005: 72). However, a distinction was in deciding how best to reconcile notions of 'competition' with the ameliorative function of education, to level the playing field in the interest of social justice (Callinicos, 2010). In essence, the commitment to a marketized system matched with a pledge to improve educational opportunities represented a 'third-way', the birth of a new 'market socialism' (Giddens, 1998) or 'more progressive settlement within a neo-liberal era' (Hodgson and Spours, 2006: 685). In this respect, New Labour's approach to post-compulsory education (now broadened to policy for 14–19 provision) stood for more than a simple 'rhetorical repackaging' of Conservative neo-liberalism. It represented the emergence of a new statist/managerialism under Prime Minister Tony Blair, yet one with a similar political and ideological persuasion in which policy-making occurred within a single political era stretching from the mid-1980s to the present (ibid.).

Such political continuities met with radical economic change throughout the 1990s and into the new millennium. As noted earlier, the new global order made particular demands on the economy and worker in ways that served to transform both (Robertson, 2005), not least in terms of the belief that a 'nation's competitiveness in global markets ultimately depends on the skills of all its people' (Coffield, 1999: 480). This gave rise to a new type of 'producer capitalism', in which economic competitiveness could no longer be achieved on price alone, but rather required an improvement in the quality of goods and services, and with this an investment in 'physical and human capital . . . [where] the development of a highly educated workforce is seen as a priority' (Brown and Lauder, 1996: 10). In this new political economy, Toffler (1990: 18) suggests that:

> knowledge itself . . . turns out to be not only the source of the highest-quality power, but also the most important ingredient of force and wealth . . . this is the key to the power shift that lies ahead, and it explains why the battle for control of knowledge and the means of communication is heating up all over the world.

The shift in the balance of power away from physical capital towards knowledge (Robertson, 2005) reflects a key point of departure in which human capital is regarded as the new 'raw material' of late-capitalist production (see also Chapter 6). This view was articulated at the beginning of New Labour's first term through the discourse of the White Paper *Excellence in Schools*:

> Investment in learning in the 21st Century is the equivalent of investment in the machinery and technical innovation that was essential to the first great industrial revolution. Then it was physical capital; now it is human capital. (DfEE, 1997a: 15)

A year later in a Green Paper (see Chapter 1 for a definition of Green Paper), *The Learning Age – a renaissance for a new Britain* (DfEE, 1998d), Prime Minister Tony Blair proclaimed that 'education is the best economic policy we have' thus endorsing the view that education is a 'mere instrument of the economy' (Coffield, 1999: 480). As the Paper suggests:

> We are in a new age – the age of information and global competition. Familiar certainties and old ways of doing things are disappearing . . . We

have no choice but to prepare for this new age in which the key to success
will be the continuous education and development of the human mind
and imagination. (DfEE, 1998d: 1.1)

The strategy deployed to address such change was both complex and
multifaceted – the politics of which extends well beyond the scope of
this chapter. However, for post-compulsory education and training there
have been a number of key structural changes that have set a context for
addressing the requirements of the 'knowledge-economy', and with this
its role in providing 'continuous education' in an 'information society'
and age of 'global competition' (Lauder et al., 2006). Under New Labour,
post-compulsory education was characterized by an even greater degree
of state 'interference', managerialism and accountability (Ball, 2007) in
which the growth of powerful unelected quangos (quasi-autonomous
non-governmental organizations) – so-called arms-length agencies –
began to multiply. Agencies such as the Learning and Skills Council
(LSC), Adult Learning Inspectorate (ALI), Qualifications and
Curriculum Authority (QCA) and Teaching and Learning Standards
Unit within the DfES produced increasing numbers of policy advisors,
mediating between elected government ministers and education
providers (Hodgson and Spours, 2006). Such complexity in the policy-
making process was further compounded by the increased autonomy of
individual education and training providers and, in some cases, new,
private ones. In the new mixed economy of public and private sector
institutions, behaviour was strongly influenced by a number of 'powerful
steering mechanisms (e.g. funding, targets and inspection)' (ibid.: 682),
regulated and delivered by quangos through 'top-down' performance
management (Ball, 2008).

The convergence of 'management, the market and performativity'
(ibid.: 52) under New Labour, served to increase the level of political
centralization and further exacerbate the 'politicization of the policy
process' (Hodgson and Spours, 2006: 682). As Tony Blair put it in the
White Paper, *Our Competitive Future* (DTI, 1998: 5), 'old fashioned state
intervention did not and cannot work', rather new-governance, managerialism and accountability should be allowed to prevail (Ball, 2007).
Thus, in a similar vein to that which had dominated the Conservative's
tenure in government, significant tensions in post-16 policy continued
to persist under New Labour. This was especially the case in terms of

making good on the ambition to sustain competition, on the one hand, while seeking to enhance collaboration (between education and training providers), on the other – as a means to provide different local opportunities and progression routes for learners. Moreover, the promise to improve economic performance was almost constantly at odds with the aim to achieve social justice. In fact, far from addressing important structural inequalities in post-compulsory provision (Tomlinson, 2008b; Ball, 2008) – as New Labour had set out to do through documents such as *Learning to succeed: a new framework for post-16 learning* [DfEE, 1999a], which had attempted to focus on 'those in greatest need', or indeed, provide assistance through the introduction of the Educational Maintenance Grants for 16–18 year olds from 2004 onwards [Pring, 2005: 72]) – a culture of heightened accountability and managerialist policies consistently undermined considerations of justice. The imposition of targets, scrutiny and surveillance upon *individuals* made them responsible for *their* own learning, and for the continuous improvement of skills to ensure *their* employability in the 'knowledge economy'. In this respect, New Right policy on individualism became much more deep-rooted under New Labour, in which it became 'not the symbol of our unfinished development, but a guarantee of our permanent inadequacy' (Illich and Verne, 1976: 13), with yet greater emphasis on individuals, their skills and the value of human capital theory.

The remainder of this chapter will focus on the two perhaps most enduring and often contentious strands of the post-compulsory education debate: the 'skills revolution' and reform of A-levels, both of which relate to the historical thread of this chapter. The skills revolution can be traced to the abovementioned FEU's *Basis for Skills* (FEU, 1979), and then followed in subsequent debates throughout the 1980s and 1990s in CBI literature (CBI, 1989; 1993). In both cases, the underlying argument for the introduction of a 'skills revolution' was based on a series of international studies showing that the UK economy was falling behind its European competitors in Organisation for Economic Cooperation and Development (OECD) comparisons (Green, 1997). Furthermore, there was a lingering view that a narrow and overly academic 16–19 curriculum served to compound poor-workforce skills (Johnson, 2004), and thus failed adequately to prepare young people for the modern workplace; still less during times of economic recession or in the midst of rising youth unemployment. At the same time, an erstwhile but tenuous view prevailed that such skills might actually link the different qualifications tracks (DfEE, 1997c; Raffe et al., 1998); however, fundamentally, 'there was a commonly held assumption, supported by human capital theory, that raising the level of skills and qualifications within the population would contribute directly to increased productivity and economic competitiveness' (Hodgson and Spours, 2002: 31) – though, of course, some like Wolf (2002; 2004; 2007) continue to challenge this view.

Nevertheless, various reports throughout the 1980s and 1990s published by HMI, SEAC, National Council for Vocational Qualifications (NCVQ), NCC, Further Education Unit (FEU) and the Training Agency (TA) all recommended that core or key skills (the semantics of which spawned yet another debate) be integrated into vocational *and* academic qualifications (i.e. A-levels), for the sake of the nation's future economic success (Hodgson and Spours, 2002). Moreover, under New Labour, 25 Sector-Skills Councils were set up to replace the old National Training Organisations, in which they became the 'lynchpins of a centrally planned, supply-driven training system' (Wolf, 2007: 113), demonstrating the specific skills required by employers and the sector as a whole of the education process. However, due to the practical difficulties associated with the implementation of skills in all qualifications post-16, and a feeling that A-levels might effectively dilute standards, such key/core skills were quickly exiled to the realm of vocational education, notably GNVQs. The outcome of *Curriculum 2000* served only to confirm the ambiguity around New Labour's appeal to 'key skills for all', and thereby exacerbate the long history of academic/vocational divisions in the English system.

Despite this fact the contradictory and cyclical nature of education policy meant that it was not long before a similar crisis in skills emerged once again (Johnson, 2004). In 2003, the White Paper, *21st Century Skills Realising our Potential: Individuals, Employers, Nation,* was published jointly by the DfES, Department of Trade and Industry and Department for Work and Pensions (DfES/DTI/DWP, 2003). Much like the earlier CBI versions that had sought to 'revolutionize' skills, the White Paper made yet another appeal for a 'skills revolution', focusing upon *individuals'* needs, with the aim to provide a broader framework of relevant skills matched to employers' needs (Pring, 2005). Like its predecessors, this document attempted to reinforce the value of functional numeracy and literacy (identified in the Moser Report, 1999 and later conceived as 'communication') and ICT as core skills, along with a range of wider process-related, though often marginal social and inter-personal skills, including 'working with others', 'learning and performance' and 'problem solving'. Critically, however, whereas previously policy to enhance such skills was presented as a matter of generating favourable 'supply-side' conditions, orchestrated by the various 'quangos of central government, the Leitch (2006) review was unequivocal in stressing the importance of a demand-led system inspired by employers (Wolf, 2007). Yet, in practice this amounted to little more than 'a whole network of additional quangos' (ibid.: 116).

Pause and ponder

The question of what 'skills' can be counted as 'economically valuable' in an evolving global economy remains contested in the context of post-compulsory education and training. With this in mind, answer the following questions:

(1) Does the ambition to develop core 'skills' promote a view of 'recognition' or 'deficit-reduction' in relation to the learner?
(2) How does the emphasis on 'economically valuable skills' enhance or impair critical thinking about the broader aims and purposes of education?

Tomlinson Report

Coinciding with the publication of the White Paper *21ˢᵗ Century Skills Realising Our Potential*, the government commissioned a Working Group to review 14–19 qualifications, chaired by Mike Tomlinson (Working Group, 2004). The Working Group emerged following the so-called A-level crisis in 2002, in which there had been accusations of unethical practice and grade-fixing (especially in the determination of coursework grades). The Working Group consulted with thousands of young people, educationalists, policy makers and professionals to develop proposals for a unified and multi-levelled diploma system, replacing A-levels and creating a fusion between academic and vocational forms of study. The new framework would serve to encourage greater participation and retention, along with enhanced choice and flexibility, through more inclusive and progressive curricula (Pring, 2005). If followed, the ideas of Tomlinson would build upon the historical debate that had taken place since the late 1980s, culminating in the publication of the *British Baccalaureate,* noted earlier (Finegold et al., 1990).

However, in 2005 the New Labour Government published a White Paper, *14–19 Education and Skills* (DfES, 2005), which rather than following the proposals of the Working Group as first anticipated, instead entirely disregarded the proposition of an over-arching diploma. Here responsibility for the proposed vocational route diploma was given over 'to employers via the Sector Skills Councils' (Keep, 2005: 538). The idea of abandoning A-levels once and for all as a means to create a more flexible, inclusive and equitable system of post-compulsory education and training had, in the end, failed miserably. Just like all previous attempts at reform it had fallen at the last hurdle; in this case, the New Labour Government concerned with political popularity during the pre-election period became nervous at the prospect of ditching the A-level 'gold-standard'. As Hodgson and Spours (2006: 685) note, 'the post-Tomlinson 14–19 . . . settlement of 2005–2006 can be seen to represent a clearer line of continuity with the previous administration than may be evident in other policy fields'. To this extent, 14–19 policy under New Labour was virtually indistinguishable from the neo-conservative arm of the political New Right. Thus, one wonders why the initial ideological commitment to social inclusion was eventually displaced by the inertia of neo-liberal reform.

From New Labour to Coalition . . . and so the cycle continues

In the inaugural year of the Conservative/Liberal Democrat Coalition, it may yet be too soon to comment on the impact of government policy on post-compulsory education and training. However, early indications would suggest the new administration is intent on simplifying and reforming vocational education in order to improve provision, just six years after Tomlinson's proposals were roundly rejected by New Labour. The commissioning of the Wolf Report (Wolf, 2011) to review vocational education, in the conspicuous absence of academic reform, is surely no accident. As Secretary of State for Education, Michael Gove, remarks in the foreword to the Wolf Report:

> Since Prince Albert established the Royal Commission in 1851 policy-makers have struggled with our failure to provide young people with a *proper technical and practical education* of a kind that other nations can boast. 160 years later the same problems remain. Our international competitors boast more robust manufacturing industries. Our *technical education* remains weaker than most other developed nations. And, in simple terms, our capacity to generate growth by making things remains weaker. (Gove, 2011: emphasis added, cited in Wolf, 2011: 4)

Paradoxically, it is interesting to note that while the virtues of high-quality vocational education are fully endorsed throughout the Report, and further, positively touted as a means of entering 'secure employment or higher-level education and training', still the Report recommends that all young people be required to study a core of academic subjects until they are 16 (Wolf, 2011: 8). Indeed, we are told that 'good levels of English and Mathematics continue to be the most generally useful and valuable vocational skills on offer. They are a necessary precondition for access to selective, demanding and desirable courses, whether these are "vocational" or "academic"; and they are rewarded directly by the labour market throughout people's careers' (ibid.: 10). The disclosure of an openly 'selective' system of post-compulsory education is in one sense admirable, but in fact no more than what most people have recognized for a very long time. The critique of existing low-level vocational qualifications, which are said to have little to no market labour value is underscored with the claim that 'in recent years, both academic and vocational education in England have been bedevilled by well-meaning attempts to pretend that everything is worth the same as everything else. Students and families all know this is nonsense' (ibid.: 9).

   In the present scramble to address the collapse of the youth labour market and involve business and industry more fully – by altering funding systems and offering subsidies to employers who provide higher quality apprenticeships with an element of general education – it is clear the review is intent on moving well beyond the piecemeal, 'supply-side' solutions that have dominated the sector for the last 30 years. The recommendation that vocational qualifications be removed from performative league tables is yet a further step away from neo-liberalism, but one that nevertheless falls short of Finegold et al.'s (1990) proposals and, indeed, those of Tomlinson (Working Group, 2004), for whom change represented the entire system of post-compulsory education, vocational *and* academic. In this latter respect, it is perhaps already clear that the tradition of inequality which has persisted in English education for more than a century is likely to go unchallenged. If such a situation transpires then will it emerge that education has failed in at least two distinct senses, both as a means to address the economic imperative and as a panacea to virtuous social policy? Only time will tell.

Pause and ponder

Can you think of any examples in the modern workplace in which vocational qualifications would be regarded superior by employers compared with academic credentials?

Taking account of recent changes in economy and society, what vision of post-compulsory education and training do you see for the future?

Further reading

Hodgson, A. and Spours, K. (2006) 'An analytical framework for policy engagement: the contested case of 14–19 reform in England', *Journal of Education Policy,* 21(6): 679–96.

Pring, R. (2005) 'Labour government policy 14–19', *Oxford Review of Education,* 31(1): 71–85.

Wolf, A. (2007) 'Round and round the houses: The Leitch review of skills', *Local Economic,* 22(2): 111–17.

Wolf, A. (2011) *Review of Vocational Education – The Wolf Report,* London: DFE.

6 Economics of Education

Introduction

Over the course of the last 40 years the relationship between education and the economy has become inseparably interwoven. Education is no longer regarded a public service or 'free good', as originally conceived in the radical reforms of the post-war settlement. It is now seen as 'big-business' (Pring, 2004), and one that continues to develop rapidly under the influence of neo-liberal politics and the evolving structural relationship between the economy and the state. In this chapter, we examine the political formation of education policy of successive modern governments, and explore the increasing role of market solutions in public policy, in particular the intrusion of economics in state education. We consider how the apparent conversion in capitals from Keynesianism to neo-liberalism under the strong influence of globalization throughout the 1970s and 1980s served not only as a catalyst for economic change but also the radical reconfiguration of education policy, including its recent alignment with human capital theory. Following a more general contextualization of educational reform, we present a set of genealogies of policy discourse in higher education, tracing the various moves, continuities and changes in policy-making where, over the last 15 years, widespread systemic and institutional change has taken place (Ertl and Wright, 2008). We analyse how neo-liberal policy imperatives in higher education (Deem, 2004) have led to a radical marketization of the sector, and, with this, an equally radical emphasis on commercial activity, the commodification of knowledge and creation of so-called university 'products' (Garratt and Hammersley-Fletcher, 2009). In particular, we consider how the rapid and unprecedented expansion of higher education in England (David, 2010), reflected in the policy drive to ensure that 40 per cent of the workforce will acquire Level 4 qualifications by 2020 (Fuller and Heath, 2010), has produced marked divisions between the more and less well-off, and created an inequitable system in which the virtue of welfare-capitalism has been seriously compromised.

Towards the 'competition state': The demise of the Keynesian National Welfare State

As noted elsewhere in Chapters 1 and 5, there has been a seismic shift in the landscape of the political economy in England since the early 1970s where a conjunction of crises – financial, economic, social and political – has conspired to render the Keynesian National Welfare State (KNWS) virtually redundant. The global oil shock of the early 1970s, coupled with chronic patterns of economic and financial instability and periods of deep recession, served to exacerbate a wide range of social, political and economic tensions across the system. During the late 1960s and 1970s, accelerating inflation *and* mass unemployment (Callinicos, 2010) confounded Keynesian economists, where alongside rising taxation costs, a condition of 'stagflation' was produced, leading to a devaluation of the economy and subsequent deep recession. Notions of ungovernability (including state/union conflict), 'demographic change, inequality, rigidity, changing national identities, family instability, movements of capital, ecological problems, etc.' (Ball, 2007: 4), provided further tangible evidence that Keynesianism had failed and become a 'hindrance to international competitiveness' (ibid.: 5), where it was now widely regarded as economically and politically untenable.

The ineffectiveness of the KNWS to regulate the economic system was based upon its well-documented failure to deal with recurring patterns of crisis in the capitalist business cycle. Yet, as Gamble (2009) explains, 'there have always been debates . . . about whether the fundamental cause of capitalist crisis was overproduction or underconsumption. Was the problem that profits were too low to continue expanding production, or was it that there was insufficient demand to buy the products?' (ibid.: 47). The Keynesian solution to the 'restless dynamism' (ibid.) of capitalism, and its characteristic peaks and troughs, is a project of state intervention – a series of economic policies intended to suppress such booms and slumps through a range of fiscal measures (i.e. macro-economic policy in the form of government spending and/or taxation), as well as regulatory interventions to address potentially harmful fluctuations in the over-accumulation of capital. Yet, as Callinicos (2010: 37) reminds us, for Keynes, capital accumulation (the investment of capital in labour, machinery, technology and money dealing as a means to produce 'surplus-value', i.e. profitability) is 'one of the defining features of a modern capitalist economy . . . it amounts to taking a bet on the future, a bet whose chances of success cannot be calculated'. This would suggest that instability and uncertainty are inherent features of capitalism, and so inevitably incapable of being managed in any complete sense (the financial crisis of 2007–08 is a case in point). The combined effect of the inflationary expansions and employment-creating contractions that were characteristic of the mid- to late 1970s paved the way for a liberal renaissance: the rise of neo-liberal capitalism.

The ideological work of the New Right, which presents a radical coalition of neo-liberal free-market thinking and individual liberty coupled with traditional shades of neo-conservatism, has been dealt with elsewhere in this book (see, for example, Chapters 1, 4 and 5). Throughout the late 1970s and 1980s, neo-liberalism drew upon a number of influential thinkers, including Frederick von Hayek, Milton Friedman and Robert Nozick (1974). For current purposes, however, it is Hayek's work, resting on 'a critique of socialism, statism and Keynesianism' (Ball, 1990: 35), that is perhaps most relevant to the analysis of the impact of economic change upon the nature and purpose of education policy.

Hayek's work was fundamentally wedded to the economic principle of free-market, *laissez-faire* capitalism. This meant that, unlike Keynes, Hayek believed that during periods of economic and financial crisis 'the state should do nothing to prevent the bust, apart from moderating the expansion of credit' (Callincos, 2010: 44) through the prudent application of monetary (rather than fiscal) policy and judicious control of interest rates (e.g. higher interest rates would increase the cost of borrowing, making it less attractive and so reduce the circulation of money in the economy). The spirit of minimal state intervention and displacement of central planning was enthusiastically adopted by the Conservative Party's opposition in the mid-1970s, under the leadership of Margaret Thatcher. When the Tories finally came to power in 1979, the full weight of Hayek's neo-liberal political and ideological framework was applied to the domestic economy. This led to the privatization of nationalized industries, support for the unfettered freedom of the individual as an economically rational and autonomous agent – for example, through the move to install 'inviolable private property rights at the heart of the social order' (Harvey, 2010: 233), via the sale of corporation housing – and explicit reinforcement of the sovereignty of free-market enterprise and competition, propagated across all sectors of society. Choice became a celebrated concept in a system in which the allocation of goods and services was determined by a quasi-market, partially free from state interference.

Pause and ponder

A society pursuing market policies sustained by competition and 'choice' is one that is arguably reserved for privileged choosers (Thrupp and Tomlinson, 2005).

Consider this statement and answer the following questions:

(1) Is the concept of 'choice' freely available to all those who want it?

(2) In the statement above, what do you understand by the term 'privileged choosers'?

(3) Who are the likely winners and losers in a marketized education system?

Neo-liberal economic policy and state education

A further rolling-back of the state emerged throughout the 1980s, when the Conservative Government introduced free-market principles to the apparatus of state education. This was manifested in the question of how, and on what basis education should attend to the needs of the political economy? The response relied predictably upon the virtue of neo-liberalism and, with it, upon the new autonomous individuals: the consumer and the parent. In general terms, the beginning of this trend can be traced to the 1980 Education Act in which, perhaps for the first time, improved parental choice was actively promoted. However, this reflected only one aspect of a much broader political agenda of choice, where a whole series of charters emerged across different areas of the public sector. These included transport and patients' charters, as well as two parents' charters in 1991 and 1994, extending parental choice and rights in education. The latter came to fruition in the way parents were allowed to express preferences for schools and also set up appeals committees as a means to challenge a malign or unfavourable circumstance, in which, for example, their child's entry to a (preferred) school may have been refused. This privileging of the parent as sovereign consumer was further reinforced in the middle of the decade in which a Green Paper on *Parental Influence at School* (DES, 1984) – leading to the Education Act 1986 – sought to extend the representation of parents on school governing bodies, from two, as required by the 1980 Act, to a maximum of five elected parent governors (Tomlinson, 2008b).

In political and economic terms such moves reinforced the neo-liberal pledge to roll-back the state by blunting the power of LEAs to intervene in the running of schools, which were now becoming increasingly locally managed through the decisions of the parent/consumer. This is significant to the development of policy in higher education, for it occasioned the rise of what Ball (2008: 45–6: original emphasis) refers to as a '*new moral environment*' and '*culture of self-interest*', in which the creation of education markets opened the door to intensive competition in the public sector, encouraging 'schools, colleges and universities to recruit students in order to maximize their "income"', and thus their internal well-being. The new ethic of '*survivalism*' produced a transformation in the education system from what was originally a public service based on notions of egalitarianism and social justice to a system of values in which considerations of efficiency, marketability and open competition prevailed, with schools, colleges and universities competing aggressively for demand in local, regional and national (and sometimes even international) marketplaces. Ethically this meant that educational institutions were no longer motivated by working cooperatively, especially in the case of schools and colleges, but rather in direct competition, with teachers and lecturers doubling as business '*entrepreneurs*' within their own institutions.

The introduction of the ERA (1988) was perhaps the most profound piece of legislation and policy reform of the neo-liberal era. Not only was it symbolic of a shift further to the political right, but it signalled an even greater commodification and confusion of 'social relationships with exchange relationships' (Ball, 1990: 87) through the implementation of 'open enrolment' and local management of schools. In this new privatized regime, schools would be funded per capita, in terms of pupil numbers, who were now reduced to a 'form of exchange between parents and schools' (ibid.: 86). On this simple equation, the greater number of pupils schools were able to attract, the more money they received and vice versa, and so the power and monopoly of LEA influence on state schooling was effectively reduced, as authorities would no longer allocate pupils to schools. As Jones (2003: 107) notes:

> Conservative legislation sought to drive neo-liberal principles into the heart of public policy. An emphasis on cost reduction, privatisation and deregulation was accompanied by vigorous measures against the institutional bases of Conservatism's opponents, and the promotion of new forms of public management. The outcome of these processes was a form of governance in which market principles were advanced at the same time as central authority was strengthened.

Such direct and decisive centralization of authority is best represented through the government's move to control funding on the basis of schools becoming more effective brokers of their own competitive advantage and individual success. The introduction of examination league tables in 1992, for example, to supply market information to parents as a means to compare the performance of state schools, provided an essential basis for choice making (Ball, 2008). Schools were thus now not only operating as independent spending units with devolved budgets, but paradoxically as quasi-autonomous businesses under a political regime of increasing centralization and state control. In many ways such developments represented the beginning of what has been referred to as the 'competition state' (Jessop, 2002: 199) in which there has been a 'redrawing of the public-private divide' through the partial privatization and commodification of pupils, and with students reconfigured as 'products' of education. In this prevailing context, competition between institutions is regarded *de facto* as the principal means of raising standards in education, as schools, colleges and universities vie to enhance quality through results and further improve their position in the educational marketplace. In many ways, the radical transformation of state schooling represents the centrepiece of hegemonic neo-liberal reform within education, and as such is vitally important in helping us understand the environment within which change in higher education has taken place. It provides not only a useful perspective on the scale of change sector-wide, but an important embryonic view of what higher education would later become under New Labour and, more latterly, the Coalition Government. With these issues in mind, we turn now to analyse the beginning of the neo-liberal settlement in higher education.

The development of higher education into the 1990s

A seminal 'move' in the development of higher education policy emerged in 1985 with the Green Paper – *The Development of Higher Education into the 1990s* (DES, 1985b), followed subsequently with the White Paper *Higher Education: Meeting the Challenge* (DES, 1987b). The Green Paper was important for a number of related reasons, notably that it arrived in the aftermath of the Great Debate (see also Chapters 1, 4 and 5), which flagged the importance of education meeting the needs of industry and commerce and also that it emerged as part of a broader set of neo-liberal educational reforms with the aim of transforming education sector wide:

> The economic performance of the United Kingdom since 1945 has been disappointing compared to the achievements of others. The Government believes that it is vital for our higher education to contribute more effectively to the improvement of the performance of the economy . . . unless the country's economic performance improves, we shall be even less able than now to afford many of the things that we value most – including education. (DES, 1985b: 3)

The aim to make education more instrumentally focused was later supported in *Meeting the challenge* (DES, 1987b), which overlaps with Chapter 5 on post-compulsory education and training, as well as the broader transformation of state education reported elsewhere in the book. In the first instance, this Green Paper argues that unless there is an increase in the supply of students of 'suitable quality' emerging from schools and colleges, coupled with an increase in interest from employers through the 'sponsorship of able students at universities and polytechnics', then improvements are unlikely to be made in producing 'appropriately qualified manpower' (DES, 1985b: 3). In fact, the link between higher education, business and industry could not be expressed more emphatically:

> Higher education establishments need to be concerned with attitudes to the world outside higher education . . . and to beware of 'anti-business' snobbery . . . the future health of higher education – and its funding from public *and private sources – depends significantly upon its own success in generating the qualified manpower the country needs . . . there is a growing concern that higher education does not always respond sufficiently to changing economic needs. This may be due in part to disincentives to change within higher education, including over-dependence on public funding . . .* (ibid.: 4; 6: emphasis added)

Of particular note to the development of higher education policy is the prevailing view of alternative funding mechanisms and future income streams. The turn towards a 'competition state' noted above is already implanted in the discourse (see Chapter 1 for an explanation of 'discourse') of 'changing economic needs', in which higher education is identified as being slow to respond to change in the face of counter-vailing disincentives. Moreover, the prevailing view of an 'over-reliance on public funding' in higher education marks the genesis for what follows later, under New Labour and beyond in the Browne Review (of which, more later). Such strong neo-liberal sentiments, supported in the view that higher education institutions should become more entre-preneurial and fundamentally business savvy, is captured further in the perspective that 'the Government would like to see even greater vitality and flexibility' within higher education. So, while universities are regarded as 'the principal guardians of pure academic excellence and the main sources of creative research', they are not seen as typical of 'the paradigm for higher education as a whole' (ibid.: 5). Indeed, back in the 1980s 'polytechnics and other institutions' were believed to 'have a distinctive responsibility to prepare people for a wide range of activities, [including] provision for adult and continuing education' (ibid.). This resonates strongly with the notion of a two-tier system of education not so dissimilar from that examined in Chapter 5 on post-compulsory education (and which has gained some momentum in the Coalition Government's recent proposals – of which, more later), and also signals the beginning of a journey to widen access and partici-pation to a more vocationally relevant higher education (DES, 1987b).

The twin move to strengthen education's link with the economy while also generating wider access to higher education formed the conceptual basis of *Higher Education: meeting the challenge* (DES, 1987b). This gave political sanction to the discourse of 'flexibility', in which new vocationally oriented degrees began to emerge at the same time as academic disci-plines became less dominant. In many ways this represented the beginning of a double movement to enhance efficiency *and* quality in higher education simultaneously – a policy that would later become enshrined within the Higher Education Quality Council (HEQC), following the publication of the 1991 White Paper *Higher Education: a new framework*. In the meantime, the proliferation of new degree programmes matched with increasingly flexible and imaginative modes of study could be seen sympathetically to align with the rhetoric of post-Fordism (see also Chapter 5), in which the impact of globalization coupled with increasing competition from external foreign markets served to create a new demand for 'human-capital' in the late-capitalist economy.

The concept of 'human capital' can be traced to the self-same title of Becker's seminal work (1964), in which he argued that people's knowledge and skills represent a form of capital capable of generating income just like a 'bank account, one hundred shares of IBM, [or] assembly lines' (Becker, 1993: 15, cited in Wolf, 2004: 317). Accordingly, in the neo-liberal regime, it is the added value of human beings rather than physical machinery *per se* that creates a competitive 'edge', and further fosters the development of new knowledge, skills and the flourishing of the entrepreneurial spirit. In turn, this generates an economy that is increasingly dependent upon knowledge – a 'knowledge economy' of scientific and technological innovation – which further aids the development of 'vitality and flexibility' in a rapidly changing global marketplace (Brown and Lauder, 1996). Correspondingly, notions of 'flexibility' are matched with the evolving vocational discourse of 'flexible specialisation' in which modern graduates are expected to be multi-skilled, more responsive and adaptable (in fact, 'employable') in conditions of ongoing social and economic change.

In addition, students are expected to have greater political awareness of the impact of increasing numbers entering into higher education generating a problem of escalating tuition fees. Interestingly, it was the Green Paper (DES, 1985b) that first drew our attention to the issue of 'whether arrangements less onerous to the taxpayer might be justified', suggesting that 'a greater financial engagement on the part of students would cause them to take greater care over their choice of study' (DES, 1985b: 15). This provided the genesis of a debate that is highly pertinent to contemporary higher education policy and politics – that human capital of the future will need to be more responsive to changing economic circumstances and that *individuals* will take greater responsibility for decisions of personal investment, both for making rationally economic choices and in sharing the burden of cost.

Pause and ponder

Look at the DfE website and find the national statistics for 'Participation Rates in Higher Education': www.education.gov.uk/rsgateway/DB/SFR/index.shtml; also check out: http://data.gov.uk/dataset/participation_rates_in_higher_education_-_academic_years.

Then examine the HEFCE website for 'Trends in young participation in higher education': www.hefce.ac.uk/pubs/hefce/2010/10_03/

Consider these trends and statistics and answer the following questions:
(1) What has happened to participation rates in higher education since the late 1990s?
(2) How can such change be viewed both positively and negatively in the context of lifelong learning?
(3) Given the recent scale of change is it realistic to expect higher education to be publicly funded in the future?
(4) Imagining this were the case, what are the likely implications of an increase in public funding in higher education for future economic policy?

Human capital formation: A theory of false assumptions?

The political discourse of education for economic growth, and its assumed dependency on the role of human capital formation, can be linked directly to the impact of global competition upon the economic performance of OECD countries in the late-twentieth century. According to Wolf et al. (2006: 535), the notion of improved 'economic performance . . . has been informed by a rather simplistic version of human capital theory' in which the development of the nation's skills has come 'to be regarded as both a critical, and a sure-fire, way of improving productivity'. Thus, in a similar vein to the rhetoric of the Green Paper (DES, 1985b), various governments, dating from the early 1980s to the current moment, have actively promoted employability policies (Brown et al., 2003) on the strength of OECD comparisons and the much publicized view that human capital formation and lifelong learning are vital to sustained economic growth. More especially so in a world in which the 'increased pace of globalisation and technological change' are said to have created 'serious deficiencies in skills and competencies in the . . . labour force' (OECD, 2004: 2–3). The very idea that the 'welfare of individuals and . . . competitive advantage of nations . . . depend[s] on the knowledge, skills and entrepreneurial zeal of the workforce' (Brown et al., 2003: 122), represents an interesting political turn, for it marks the beginning of a trend in which economic policy is strategically presented as responsible social policy. This is taken as 'good' not only for the aspirations of the *individual* and future economic prosperity of the nation, but as a means to enhance public welfare and corporate social responsibility.

Ironically however, as Wolf (2002; 2004) argues, there is scarce empirical evidence to support the view that education can improve productivity and economic performance, even though governments since the early 1980s have enthusiastically proceeded on this assumption. For example, following the Green Paper (DES, 1985b), the Conservatives released two White Papers: one announcing their plans to 'to improve and develop the education and training system . . . [in] response to the rising demand from employers for more and higher level skills to meet the growing challenge from overseas competitors in world markets' (DES, 1991a: 1); and a second proposing a new framework for higher education (DES, 1991b). Another six years on, and Tony Blair's New Labour Government announced that 'investment in learning in the twentieth century is the equivalent of investment in the machinery and technical innovation that was essential to the first great industrial revolution. Then it was physical capital; *now it is human capital*' (DfEE, 1997c: 15: emphasis added). Elsewhere, under New Labour, we heard that 'learning is the key to prosperity. Investment in human capital will be the foundation of success in the knowledge-based economy of the twenty-first century' (DfEE, 1998d: 1). Quite apart from the idea of whether education can bring about improved economic growth, the latter contains a further questionable assumption: that formal learning, realized and measured via qualification targets, can serve as an accurate 'proxy for skills acquisition' (Wolf et al., 2006: 538). Indeed, there is little empirical evidence to support the claim that improved qualifications, creatively interpreted as improved skills, are able to contribute towards economic policy objectives (ibid.). In fact, where evidence does exist it is reported to be ambiguous and contradictory (Keep and Mayhew,

2004), and so, in the end, while the workforce may be much better qualified, we ask whether, in fact, it is any better skilled.

Ponder and Pause

'Graduate gloom as 83 students apply for every vacancy':
> www.telegraph.co.uk/education/8602101/Graduate-gloom-as-83-students-apply-for-every-vacancy.html
> www.prospects.ac.uk/usa_job_market.htm

Follow the links above, read the articles and answer the following questions:
(1) Why is competition so fierce for graduate level jobs, at home and abroad?
(2) Do qualifications automatically assure the reward of higher salaries for well qualified graduates?

The National Committee of Inquiry into Higher Education – Higher education in the learning society

A year before New Labour's election victory in 1997, a series of working groups were commissioned to conduct a National Inquiry into Higher Education in the United Kingdom. The committee, chaired by Ron Dearing, received consent from all political parties to examine, and further make recommendations on 'how the purposes, shape, structure, size and funding of higher education, including support for students, should develop to meet the needs of the United Kingdom over the next 20 years' (Dearing, 1996b: 3). The extensive report, comprising some 23 chapters, 466 pages and 93 recommendations begins by declaring that 'the purpose of education is life-enhancing: it contributes to the whole quality of life . . . In the next century, the economically successful nations will be those which become learning societies: where all are committed, through effective education and training, to lifelong learning' (ibid.: 7). A key theme throughout is linked to the expansion of higher education in which 'people in all walks of life' (ibid.: 9), regardless of background, will recognize the 'need to continue in education and training throughout their working lives' (ibid.). The catchphrase 'lifelong learning' is thus intended to capture and respond to 'the pace of change in the work-place', which 'will require people to re-equip themselves, as new knowledge and new skills are needed for economies to compete, survive and prosper' (ibid.). That higher education should respond to the needs of the economy is affirmed on the somewhat dubious view that 'experience suggests that the long-term demand from industry and commerce will be for higher levels of education and training for their present and future workforce' (ibid.). As noted above, the concept of increased certification is questionable as a means to enhance productivity (Wolf, 2004), even though 'the economic imperative is . . . to resume growth', and the means to achieve this is by increasing levels of participation in higher education to '40 per cent or beyond' (Dearing, 1996b: 9). As Wolf (2004: 330) goes on to argue, 'if chasing quantity reduces quality, societies can actually end up worse off than before in terms of the human-capital formation they seek'.

Higher education for the twenty-first century and beyond

New Labour's response to the Dearing Report (1996b) was articulated in the White Paper *Higher Education for the 21st Century* (DfEE, 1998e), which emphasized the increasing importance of higher education's role and 'contribution to the economy and its responsiveness to the needs of business' (DfEE, 1998e: 3). The principal means to achieve this – by 'increasing participation and widening access' – appears in continuation with the outgoing Conservative Government's stance on higher education policy (DES, 1987b). However, the emphasis on ensuring a positive entitlement for 'groups who are under-represented in higher education, including people with disabilities and young people from semi-skilled or unskilled family backgrounds and from disadvantaged localities' (DfEE, 1998e: 3), provides an interesting point of departure, with a different rhetorical appeal towards inclusion, egalitarianism and the notion of social democracy. Thus, in contrast to the Conservatives, New Labour appeared committed, in their first term at least, 'to the principle that anyone who has the capability for higher education should have the opportunity to benefit from it and [we] will therefore lift the cap on student plans imposed by the last government' (ibid.: 5).

Any initial move towards inclusion and social justice in higher education policy- making, however, was simultaneously met with the view that such policy should also make more economic impact. Here, the apparent tensions are not so much contradictory but quite typical of New Labour thinking, and the dual approach offered by the 'third-way'. In this sense, the value of marketization as a model for economic success can be seen to coexist alongside enhanced state regulation. This is intended to address the corrosive effects of market forces upon the most disadvantaged groups within society. However, despite such rhetoric, we suggest the market reigns supreme. From an economic perspective, for example, the Department for Education and Employment invested £3 million in the year 1998–99 in funding the 'systematic interaction between higher education and business on skills development', and to develop regional networks to facilitate links to employability and work experience (ibid.: 35). Such links to 'employability', 'human capital theory' and the 'knowledge economy', as well as the more general debate concerning the 'skills revolution', have served to transform higher education in the most radical way.

> ### Pause and ponder
>
> The concept of 'lifelong learning' has led to the intractable view that qualification-bearing learning is a 'good thing' (Coffield, 1999).
>
> Think about this statement and answer the following questions:
> (1) What is your understanding of lifelong-learning?
> (2) In a climate of enhanced 'choice', what are the likely consequences of choosing to opt-out of lifelong learning?
> (3) Is it possible to favour lifelong learning while at the same time reject qualification-bearing learning?

Over the last 20 years, the exponential growth and so-called massification – (the move from an elite to a mass system) of higher education (Henkel, 2000; Jarvis, 2000; Morley, 2003; Barr, 2004; HEFCE 2004) has gathered considerable momentum across the globe, literally transforming the sector, as the move to 'widen participation' continues apace. Higher education institutions 'are constantly in motion' and 'change is a permanent condition, with universities constantly responding to external and internal demands' (Delanty, 2008: 126). The resultant structural effect has produced not only greater numbers of students from a wider variety of backgrounds entering into higher education, but, in fact, greater political centralization as the orchestration of what counts as 'good university education' has become increasingly state-managed.

In this important respect, while the sector has seen a manifold increase in the number of higher education providers, and further proliferation of taught programmes with ever more flexible forms of study, at the same time institutions have become more accountable to central government policy. This brings us to our second point; that the primacy of human capital formation has served to produce a state-informed agenda in which higher education is inspired paradoxically by 'government ideas on how to promote productivity' (Wolf et al., 2006: 540). It is not, as economic sense would have it, a vision of education that is authentically 'demand-led', inspired from the bottom up and thus shaped by the economic and business-related needs of employers. It is rather a system of governance inspired through networks in which centrally imposed policies actively structure notions of relevance and employability (Boden and Nedeva, 2010), and hence support the alignment of particular qualifications with the aim to improve economic growth. While on first inspection the logic of this alignment may seem economically irrational, it is, in fact, perfectly consistent with the politics of neo-liberalism, in which the purpose of state-managed intervention is entirely deliberate. In essence, it helps create the supply-side conditions under which the growth of efficient, economic activity is able to flourish and proceed unimpeded.

In this regard, the ideology of 'individualism', reinforced through the concept of choice and human capital formation under neo-liberal reform, reflects not only an 'economic turn' in education policy-making, but a direct play towards social policy, in which individuals are forced to bear the consequences and full moral responsibility of *their* choices, especially those that reject the continuous demand for improved skills and/or 'lifelong learning'. However, it is sobering to remind ourselves that as yet there is no proven correlation between increasing numbers of graduates and improved economic success (Eggins, 2003).

A further dimension of New Labour's higher education policy involved the 'commercialisation of research and knowledge' along with the launch of the 'Higher Education and Employment Development Prospectus', a venture of funded projects designed to 'make a significant contribution to promoting entrepreneurship within higher education' (DfEE, 1998e: 36). Indeed, this was a message echoed elsewhere in Tony Blair's foreword to the White Paper *Our Competitive Future – building the knowledge driven economy:*

> In Government, in business, in our universities and throughout society we must do much more to foster a new entrepreneurial spirit: equipping ourselves for the long term, prepared to seize opportunities, committed to constant innovation and enhanced performance. That is the route to commercial success and prosperity for all. We must put the future on Britain's side. (DTI, 1998: 5)

The deliberative move to combine public sector education with private sector participation became a prominent feature of the rise of the 'competition state' (Jessop, 2002) in the late 1990s and into the early twenty-first century. In economic terms it marked a significant departure in two important ways: on the one hand, a shift away from the old-fashioned model of Keynesian bureaucracy and 'big government' and on the other, a subtle distancing from Hayekian neo-liberalism, popularized under the Conservative Governments of Thatcher and Major. The 'third-way' thus came to represent a more nuanced and sophisticated form of neo-liberal economic and social policy, a form of 'market socialism' (Giddens, 1998), or, indeed, what Jessop (2002) has referred to as the 'Shumpeterian Workfare State', based on the thinking of Austrian–American economist and political scientist, Joseph Schumpeter. Ball (2007: 5–7) takes Jessop's analysis further arguing that the discourse of education policy under New Labour is characteristic of a number of Schumpeterian principles: namely, that the state has become a commissioner and monitor (rather than owner) of public services and a broker of all social and economic innovations, that the aim of public/private partnership and, hence, shared ownership is based on innovation, competitiveness and entrepreneurship and that the government has a role to play in investing in human resources to develop an entrepreneurial culture. Indeed, the discourse of innovation and entrepreneurship in higher education has produced a condition in which 'politics and business get embedded in the "texture of texts"' (Fairclough, 2000: 158), as part of the process of thinking about, and in articulating education policy. As the White Paper *The Future of Higher Education* usefully illustrates:

> Realising our vision will take time. Having presented a radical picture of a freer future, it is the duty of government to make sure that the transition is managed carefully and sensibly so that change is not destabilising. So in some areas government will want to support the way in which institutions move towards new freedoms, and develop new patterns of provision. Government also has to retain a role because it is the only body that can balance competing interests between the different stakeholders. It will also have a responsibility to intervene when universities fail to provide adequate opportunities or when access, quality or standards are at risk . . . We see a higher education sector which meets the needs of the economy in terms of trained people, research, and technology transfer . . . [and which] acknowledges and celebrates the differences between institutions as each defines and implements its own mission. (DfES, 2003b: 21–2)

Perhaps, the most radical and disruptive change in higher education policy-making under New Labour came with the restructuring of funding arrangements sector-wide. Following the recommendations of the Dearing Commission (1996) to move away from a block grant scheme towards a system in which funding follows the student, the New Labour Government adopted a formula 'based directly on the number of students enrolled' at a particular institution (DfEE, 1998e: 53). This meant that more of the funding would now follow student demand, so that in a semi-privatized environment more popular universities would eventually become richer and more financially secure. It also suggested that higher education institutions were now in direct competition with one another. This meant they had to become more marketable and business-like to appeal to an expanding base of students re-clothed as 'buying consumers'. Thus, as universities became ever more concerned about their reputation and market position, so branding and commercialization became increasingly prominent, with institutions repackaging themselves more distinctively as 'branded products' to be bought in the corporate marketplace.

In addition to radically revised funding arrangements, *Higher Education for the 21st century* introduced plans to increase the cost of tuition for undergraduate students. The Dearing Commission had recommended that students pay 'around a quarter of the average cost of a course – with the other three quarters being met from public funds'. In turn, 'the Government supported this principle' stating that 'the investment of the nation must be balanced by the *commitment of the individual*' (DfEE, 1998e: 54: emphasis added). This marked the beginning of a somewhat curious but inexorable slide towards full-time undergraduate students paying more for their university education proportionately than at any point since the post-war settlement. In 2006, for example, a system of fees was introduced in England whereby students would now be subject to a new regime of higher variable fees. In practice, over the next few years, this meant that almost all higher education institutions would eventually move towards a position of charging the maximum statutory fee of £3,225 in the year 2009/2010 – the last in New Labour's term of office. More than this, however, the seismic shift in policy linked to student fees heralded a key departure from the conception of students as 'partners' in the education business to a model in which they became fully fledged 'clients'. This prompted a revision of student expectations towards 'service provision' and 'service quality' as increasing numbers of undergraduate students with more exacting standards were now able to demand better value for money and improved returns on *their* investment (Foskett et al., 2006).

The independent review of higher education funding and student finance

In 2008, the world changed in the most dramatic fashion following the collapse of the banking system, giving rise to the 'biggest global financial crash since the Great Depression of the 1930s' (Callinicos, 2010: 2). While the move towards a fully privatized system of higher education was already in motion, and had been so since the radical reforms of the 1980s, the global financial crisis and subsequent economic meltdown threw the issue of higher education funding into sharp relief. Indeed, it served to focus attention more acutely on the economics of higher education at a time when Britain's total debt was reported to be worsening, and forecast to top £10 trillion by 2015 (Rowley, 2010). In the wake of the financial 'crash' and a new era of austerity post-2008, the then New Labour Government, just six months away from an historic election defeat, commissioned an independent review of higher education. Chaired by Lord Browne of Madingley, and comprising panel members from business and academe, the review made a strong case for further investment in higher education not only because it 'transforms the lives of individuals' but also because it 'drives innovation and economic trans-formation. Higher education helps to produce economic growth, which in turn contributes to national prosperity' (Browne Report, 2010: 14). While politically there is nothing new in the tenor of this economic argument, a key difference is contained in the view that *individuals* will now be responsible for such investment and that 'HEIs [higher education institutions] should persuade students that they should "pay" more in order to "get more"' (ibid.: 4) from their university experience. This will done by 'ensuring that students get the benefits of more competition, by publishing an annual survey of charges, looking after the interests of students when an HEI is at risk and regulating the entry of new providers' (ibid.: 11). So while on one hand higher education is regarded as highly valuable, not least because it pump-primes 'future economic growth and social mobility', on the other it is seen as desirable only in so far as individuals themselves are able to pay for it, and further 'buy' into the promise of a transformed life. According to such policy, this is a life in which 'higher status jobs' and increased earnings are guaranteed to follow (ibid.: 14). The reality, however, is that graduate level jobs are in astonish-ingly scarce supply as more graduates flood the market – currently some 83 graduates are reported to be chasing every job vacancy (Paton, 2011) – and analysts predict that 'the employment situation will cut worse before it improves, as government cutbacks hit the public sector and slow wider economic growth' (Rowley, 2011). This being the case, the clarity and assuredness with which degree level qualifications are able to secure graduate-level employment and future long-term prosperity is at best moot. At worst it is a fantasy of mythical proportions (Wolf, 2002; 2004), though, we suggest, this is only part of it.

In comparison with policy under New Labour, the Browne Report steps further towards the political right in advocating a 'direct funding relationship between student and HEI' (Browne Report, 2010: 10), albeit one that is initially closely monitored:

> The relationship between students and institutions will be at the heart of the system. We are reducing the reliance of the system on funding from Government and control by Government. Nevertheless there is an important role for regulation to look after students' interests and the ongoing public investment in higher education. We propose a new HE Council with five core responsibilities: investing in priority courses; setting and enforcing baseline quality levels; delivering improvements on the access and completion rates of students from disadvantaged backgrounds; ensuring that students get the benefits of more competition in the sector; and resolving disputes between students and institutions. (ibid.: 45)

The current system in which 'institutions are funded by HEFCE on the basis of a notional annual allocation of undergraduate places' (ibid.: 32), will transform into one where open competition is more actively encouraged between universities, and where growth in more successful institutions is promoted rather than stifled: 'Institutions will face no restrictions from the Government on how many students they can admit. This will allow relevant institutions to grow; and others will need to raise their game to respond' (ibid.: 33). The move to a more overtly marketized system is thus intended to raise the barrier on student numbers entering into particular prestigious institutions in two important ways. First, to allow all successful universities to expand and grow, much in the way that successful businesses do by selling popular products and second, to enable students from wealthier backgrounds to obtain a university education if their families are willing to pay more for an extra place – the suggestion of which stirred up a political furore, leading to a partial retraction from the Universities' Minister, David Willets (Mulholland and Vesagar, 2011).

The wholesale privatization of higher education promoted in the Browne Review, and implemented by the Coalition Government since

October 2010, has taken a further curious and problematic turn. The radical overhaul of student funding arrangements now means that universities have the freedom to charge between £6,000 and £9,000 for student tuition fees, as a means to replace lost state funding (Coughlan, 2011). While the government was initially clear to point out that only in exceptional circumstances would universities be allowed to charge the highest fee of £9,000, in practice the withdrawal of public funding has served to reinforce the sovereignty of the market, and with this focus the gaze of university vice-chancellors on 'client perceptions' of quality. In practice, it is virtually impossible *de facto* for institutions to charge any *less* than £9,000 a year for tuition fees, without at the same time implying certain degree courses are substandard, or, indeed, of lower quality than competitors charging the maximum market rate. This produces a situation in which 'with more universities than expected charging the maximum £9,000 a year for tuition, universities minister David Willetts' is seeking a way to reduce the liabilities of the government-backed Student Loans Company by turning to the UK's major banks to provide loans at preferable rates' (Boffey, 2011: 6). Sir Steve Smith, President of Universities UK and vice-chancellor of Exeter University has indicated that 'the proposal to allow banks to exploit the student market carried huge risks and could create a two-tier system', potentially allowing wealthier students to buy their way into university education (ibid.). This suggests that students from wealthier homes are able indirectly to gain a significant advantage in a privatized system over their less affluent peers.

This situation, of the more affluent benefitting over the less well off, is in danger of being replicated in relation to the stakes and relative position of universities competing in the new market environment. For example, the private university BPP has recently launched a bid to run ten publicly funded university institutions, where 'under the model, universities would control all academic decisions, while BPP would be responsible for managing the campus estate, IT support, the buying of goods and services and other "back office" roles. BPP would not hold equity in the universities' (Shepherd, 2011). The proposition of a new partnership model is as yet untested in the context of higher education, but already there are some concerns that such relations might ultimately blur accountability and hence impact negatively on educational quality.

At the time of writing, the Coalition Government's White Paper on Higher Education (BIS, 2011) had just been published, promising a free-market in higher education and strengthening the priority of competition as a means to improve quality and drive up standards. However, as Scott (2011: 2) notes it may well deliver the very opposite, for instead of one 'simple limit' being placed on 'overall student numbers, there will be three caps' – a cap for 'top' students, typically those with AAB grades at A-level, entering Russell Group universities, a cap for 'cheap' students, typically those applying to institutions that charge less than £7,000 per annum and a third cap for the rest. As Scott (ibid.) elaborates:

> the white paper promises deregulation . . . yet it is difficult to discover any significant relaxation of bureaucratic controls . . . to implement the proposals the government will have to give itself (or HEFCE) new legal powers over universities . . . far from disappearing HEFCE is to become the lead regulator. This is nationalisation with a vengeance . . . the white paper promises it promotes social mobility. Again, it does the opposite . . . it will simply lead to a further polarisation of students with 'top' universities crowded even more with 'good' students – in other words those who by and large are socially privileged enough to have attended 'good' schools (many of them private).

The driving force in the new era of austerity may well be to 'cut higher education's coat to the Treasury's tight cloth' (ibid.). However, unless the Coalition Government is quickly able to learn some important lessons from the impact and well-documented failures of neo-liberal policy-reform in state education, then it is questionable whether yet more bureaucratically regulated privatization will effectively yield the promised dividend of enhanced educational quality. While universities may well become more efficient businesses in the longer-term, whether in the end the market can deliver a high-quality, fair and sustainable system of higher education for everyone, regardless of social background, remains, at best, an open question.

Further reading

Ball, S.J. (2007) *Education Plc – Understanding Private Sector Participation in Public Sector Education*, London: Routledge.

Callinicos, A. (2010) *Bonfire of Illusions – The Twin Crises of the Liberal World,* Cambridge: Policy Press.

Tomlinson, S. (2008) *Education in a Post-Welfare Society* 2nd edn, Maidenhead: Open University Press.

Wolf, A. (2002) *Does Education Matter? Myths about Education and Economic Growth,* London: Penguin.

Globalization and Policy-borrowing

Introduction

This chapter begins by examining the nature and meaning of globalization: its characteristics, complexity and pervasive influence. Then an international, comparative stance is adopted to show that, in spite of the influence of globalization, significant differences remain in the construction of policy between different education systems. The chapter draws attention to a variety of nuanced perspectives to identify key differences in the overlapping discourses of globalization, policy-learning and policy-borrowing. Particular cases, which focus on the creation of different types of schools, curricula and the management of performance, are drawn upon to illuminate instances of policy convergence and divergence. The chapter highlights the tensions and points of resistance that impede the transfer of policy from one context to another. 'Policy networks' and 'policy entrepreneurs', are significant in the international flow of policy, and such roles are also given consideration. Through a variety of cases, the chapter contrasts the idea of 'imitation, emulation or copying' (Dale, 1999: 9) in policy (bilaterally from one country to another) with more implicit notions of globalized change.

Globalization: Definitions and its characteristics

Globalization is a widely used term that Kellner (2000: 299) suggests is a 'buzzword of the decade'. Defining globalization is not a straightforward endeavour, however, as it encompasses multiple meanings and interpretations. At the outset, one might even contemplate and deliberate whether globalization actually exists – is it tangible? Globalization might constitute an ideology, a discourse, a phenomenon, a trend, a process – or perhaps something else? Nonetheless, despite these various characterizations it is pragmatic, as a starting point, to comprehend globalization as a concept that describes the way in which the world appears increasingly as a single social system. At its broadest, globalization is associated with the increasing interconnectedness and integration of contemporary world society (Held et al., 1999) and 'the intensification of consciousness of the world as a whole' (Robertson, 1992: 8). Typically, the concept is used to interpret the vast economic, political and cultural changes that have been experienced globally, particularly since the late 1990s onwards.

In the 1960s Marshall McLuhan coined the term 'the global village' to refer to the way in which the electronics revolution had transformed time and space. Since then, 'globalization' has been utilized to explain the interconnected nature of the world and the growing interdependence of communities and countries. Burbules and Torres (2000: 12) maintain the process of globalization is evident in 'the changes in communication technologies, migration patterns, and capital flows'. McGrew (1992: 65–6) suggests:

> Globalisation refers to the multiplicity of linkages and interconnections that transcend the nation-states (and by implication the societies) which make up the modern world. It defines a process through which events, decisions, and activities on one part of the world can come to have significant consequences for individual and communities in quite distant parts of the globe.

However, Watkins and Fowler (2003: 31) contend 'developing countries have been progressively integrated into a global economy since the discovery of the New World more than five centuries ago'. Contemporary understandings of globalization arguably stem from the early 1970s and the world oil crisis that prompted important technological and economic changes (Burbules and Torres, 2000). Also, in the 1970s and 1980s there was a dramatic intensification of globalization due to shift to 'post-Fordist' methods of production (Murray, 1989) (see Chapter 5) and development of the information society, cultural globalization and post-modern culture (Harvey, 1990). Especially notable are the explosion of the 'globalization theory' and a proliferation of academic literature about globalization from the 1990s onwards. A review of relevant literature uncovers varying definitions and as these become more explanatory and encompassing the complexity of globalization becomes more apparent. Rothenberg's (2003) analysis, for instance, offers the following:

> Globalisation is the acceleration and intensification of interaction and integration among the people, companies and governments of different nations. This process has effects on human well-being (including health and personal safety), on the environment, on culture (including ideas, religion, and political systems), and on economic development and prosperity of societies across the world. (Rothenberg, 2003: 4)

Rothenberg accentuates the dynamism of globalization by emphasizing its 'intensification and acceleration'. The speeding-up aspect of globalization has been explored at length by Harvey (1990) who attributes this type of change, referred to as 'space-time compression', to the increasingly abstract activities of the global exchange of capital. Giddens' (1990) examination of 'modernity' is similar to Harvey's in terms of the connecting up of the local and the global and the increased pace and scope of change. Giddens (1990: 14) engages with the concept of 'time-space distanciation', the process by which new technologies re-organize time and space. He argues that geographical distance has changed dramatically in the modern era. The shrinking world is due to the development of Information and Communication Technologies (ICTs) whereby global communication networks, such as the internet, provide new and ever faster modes of connecting people and societies. According to Giddens (1990: 64) globalization 'stretches' the connections between different social contexts or regions resulting in 'local involvements (circumstances of co-presence) and interaction across distance (the connection of presence and absence)'.

Definitions are clearly varied and address different aspects of globalization. It is the view of globalization as an economic phenomenon, however, that best exemplifies the increasing interconnectedness and independence between nation-states, the transcendence of power above that of national boundaries and time-space compression. Hence, for some authors, the main driving force of the world's contemporary interconnectedness is due to the expansion of globalized chains of production and consumption fuelled by the expansion of neo-liberal economic thinking and practice. Economic definitions of globalization can thus be understood as the formation of internationally integrated economies characterized by openness to international trading and increasingly greater movement of capital and labour across national borders (Burbules and Torres, 2000). Capling et al. (1998) explain economic globalization as:

> The emergence of a global economy which is characterised by uncontrollable market forces and new economic actors such as transnational corporations, international banks, and other financial institutions. (Capling et al., 1998: 5)

National governments around the world have been guided by the perceptions of a global economy and post-industrialism where knowledge, information and creativity are vital for economic success. Economic prosperity is dependent on the knowledge of workers and hence there is a critical role for education in the development of 'human capital' (Williams, 2009). What has ensued is essentially a global policy discourse encompassing highly skilled, adaptable workers functioning in a knowledge economy/learning society. Whereas many nation-states (including the United Kingdom) previously based their policies on Keynesian macro-economics (see Chapter 1), state ownership and economic planning, these ideas are no longer regarded as pertinent in a world characterized by flexibility, de-regulated markets, increased insecurity and political uncertainties (Henry et al., 2008). Neo-liberalism has permeated policy-making thus globalizing the world economy and capital mobility where consequences are characterized by greater inter-dependence and instability. As such, Giddens (1994) sees the increasing role of 'action at a distance' whereby the actions that take place in one nation-state can have profound consequences for another. An example of this would be the decision of a supermarket based in the United Kingdom to stop providing free plastic carrier bags to its customers for environmental motives, but resulting in the closure of a plastic bag manufacturer in China and the loss of 20,000 jobs.

Trade has created links and interdependence between producers and consumers that are often geographically distant. These trade relation-ships can often be thought of as 'transnational' as they involve multina-tional and transnational corporations (e.g. BP, Toyota, Apple, Microsoft, Kraft), which can undermine or at least bypass inter-state relations. Similarly, supranational agencies such as: the World Bank, International Trade Organisation (ITO), International Monetary Fund (IMF), World Trade Organisation (WTO) and the OECD have arisen prominently to operate above and across national boundaries in what Rosenau (1992) refers to as 'governance without government'. Their dominance signifi-cantly weakens national power, national sovereignty and national promi-nence, a state which Castells (1997: 121) regards as the 'powerless state'. However, while relinquishing national political power on the one hand, the world's richest countries have arguably opted into and promoted supranational agencies as a means of preserving their own privileged positions within the world economy (Cerny, 1997). While the world's major economies may share a common ideological response to global problems, and to some extent cede authority to international organi-zations, it is not a case of relinquishing all political capacity. Nation-states respond in different ways in that the effects of globalization are mediated through different national societal peculiarities and idiosyn-cratic cultures (Dale, 1999). Nation-states do therefore continue to maintain their distinctiveness although, as Ball (1999: 200) points out, it is the way in which supranational agencies 'represent the accepted, collective wisdom of "the west"' that is significant.

Beck (2000a; 2000b; 2006) provides an alternative perspective; his analysis of globalization differs somewhat from those theorists who focus on the nation-state. Beck's concerns predominantly span global insecurities and the increase in risk that extend into what he refers to as the 'second age of modernity' (Beck, 2000a). He is primarily interested in what he sees as shared global problems: ecological and environmental problems and climate change; war, terrorism, armed conflict over resources and weapons of mass destruction; and issues connected to poverty, health and human rights. Beck appeals for a common awareness that leads on to a cosmopolitan consciousness of community. He argues that the problems are global and therefore cannot satisfactorily be addressed by individual nation-states. Beck thus emphasizes the desirability of transition from national to cosmopolitan society and politics:

> The question I want to put on the agenda is: how to imagine, define and analyse post-national, transnational *and* political communities? How to build a conceptual frame of reference to analyse the coming of a cosmopolitan society (behind the facade of nation-state societies) and its enemies. (Beck, 2000a: 90)

Besides the economic and political characteristics of globalization, other authors focus on its cultural and social aspects. Rizvi (2000) provides a flavour of the cultural dimensions in which globalization operates and permeates contemporary societies:

> Practices that are transcultural, emerging out of rapid flows of cultures across national boundaries, not only through global media and information technologies but also through the movement of people . . . for a range of purposes including migration, tourism, business and education. (Rizvi, 2000: 208–9)

Stiglitz (2002) offers a positive analysis in social terms:

> Globalisation has brought better health, as well as an active global civil society fighting for more democracy and greater social justice. (Stiglitz, 2002: 214)

Castells (2000), however, provides an alterative perspective to Stiglitz purporting the emergence of a 'Fourth World' which comprises:

> . . .multiple black holes of social exclusion throughout the planet. The Fourth World comprises large areas of the globe . . . it is also present

in literally every country, and every city, in this new geography of social exclusion. (Castells, 2000: 164)

Pause and ponder

Spend some time thinking about the nature and meaning of globalization. In order to come to your own judgement you might want to consider the following:

• What are the main benefits of globalization?
• What are the potential problems?

Globalization has enabled markets to expand so that we have a 'global economy', but globalization affects countries or people in different ways.

• Who benefits most from globalization?
• Who has the most to lose?

There are different theories of globalization within the literature as the extracts above show; globalization is an inexact term with multiple meanings. In terms of the drivers of globalization, the literature typically cites the influence of single causes, for example, capitalism (Wallerstein, 2011), technology (Rosenau and Singh, 2002) or political factors (Gilpin, 1992). Other authors, however, such as Giddens (1990) and Robertson (1995), suggest multiple causes to account for globalization and cite a complex set of interconnecting processes. Globalization thus remains a contested concept (Rizvi, 2004).

Homogenization and differentiation

The interconnectedness of the world via globalization simultaneously brings about homogenization (sameness) and differentiation. In terms of evidence of 'sameness' one can consider the nature of global brands, commodities and images. For example, McDonalds, Disney, Nike, Coca Cola are well known global brands; the particular symbols associated with them are widely acknowledged and their meaning understood globally. So, for instance, the bright yellow 'M' associated with McDonalds, and which is symbolic of American culture, would be instantly recognizable worldwide to anyone already familiar with it; they would immediately know that that particular icon signifies 'fast food'. Such is the power of this phenomenon that the term 'McDonaldization' was coined in 1990s by Ritzer (2008) as:

> The process by which the principles of the fast-food restaurant are coming to dominate more and more sectors of American society as well as the rest of the world. (Ritzer, 2008: 1)

McDonaldization has become incorporated in the academic and public lexicon as an 'exorable process' (Ritzer, 2008: 2) to explain the increasing homogenization and standardization across all countries where tastes and systems alike are being controlled and developed by large corporations. In a similar vein Bryman (2004) created the term 'Disneyization' of society, which is a comparable analysis of global society. There are other shared elements of life that might be considered the same worldwide too such as city life, religion, the existence of human rights and so on. However, at the same time, there is also differentiation and the re-working of the global in relation to local circumstances, what Robertson (1995) refers to as 'glocalization'. So, remaining with some of the examples given above there are country-specific menus in McDonalds designed specifically to suit particular national and cultural tastes, Italian children have renamed Disney's Mickey Mouse 'Toplino', the practice of Islam is quite different in different countries and there are different interpretations of human rights. Robertson (1995: 30) thus cautions:

> . . . it is wrong simply to read off from the global to understand what is happening locally. And it is wrong to assume the local is detached from what is happening globally; rather what is happening needs to be increasingly understood as glocalisation involving 'the simultaneity and the interpenetration of what are conventionally called the global and the local'.

As can be seen, globalization is not a homogenous, consistent or linear process – it is multifaceted. There is little consensus with respect to definitions, characteristics, explanations and influences and it has had, and can have, positive and/or negative effects on societies. In recent years globalization has been given considerable attention by theorists and education policy-makers alike and a rational question would be: what is the impact of globalization on education? Largely due to the inextricable links between the economy and education the performance of the education system is regarded as a benchmark for national economic success. It is to the relationship between globalization and education that the chapter now turns.

Globalization and education

The impact of globalization is probably the most significant challenge currently facing national education systems. Certainly, in the field of comparative and international education current literature examines the global influences that considerably and significantly challenge the sovereignty and importance of the nation-state in education. Increasingly, multi-lateral agencies such as the United Nations Educational, Scientific and Cultural Organization (UNESCO) and OECD shape, determine and mandate global educational policy debates and agendas (Resnik, 2006). Much of UNESCO's work involves information sharing and setting standards in education as a means of creating an enhanced provision of education driven by notions of equality of opportunity and as a liberal internationalist ideal (Jones, 1988). The Paris-based OECD was one of the earliest facilitators of bilateral funding for cross-national testing and comparative studies. Its Programme for International Student Assessment (PISA) surveys, undertaken every 3 years, measure literacy in reading, mathematics and science for 15-year-old students. Commission agencies produce the tests and the results provide statistical information enabling politicians and policy-makers to compare different countries' education systems and socio-economic performance. The data is often used by policy-makers to justify change or provide support for an existing policy direction (Grek, 2009).

The last survey in 2009 was undertaken by 65 countries and involved approximately 470,000 students. The Pacific Asian countries of Japan, Singapore and Korea are unfailingly at the top of the PISA rankings. In recent surveys Finnish students have consistently performed well in the PISA tests, coming out top overall and hence attracting the attention of policy-makers across the globe (Helle and Klemelä, 2010). In comparison, the performance of students in the United Kingdom has shown a notable decline in the rankings falling in 2009 to twenty-fifth place for reading, twenty-eighth place for mathematics and sixteenth place for science (Shepherd, 2010). This was after a slump in 2006 when the United Kingdom fell from seventh place to seventeenth in reading, from eighth to twenty-fourth place in mathematics (Woodward, 2007) and from fourth to fourteenth place in science (Curtis, 2007). The PISA survey and the data produced are highly esteemed internationally, and so, despite the emphasis on and investment in education by the current and former UK governments, this external and very public evaluation of the national system does not bode well for policy-makers.

Over to you . . .

Find out more about the PISA survey. Access the OECD at www.oecd.org and search for 'What PISA is'. Use the menus provided or the search function to explore:

- What PISA assesses
  - Look at the methods of assessment
  - Look at the sample questions
- What PISA produces
  - Use the menu provided to look at the rankings by country/economy

Now read:

Grek, S. (2009) 'Governing by numbers: the PISA "effect" in Europe', *Journal of Educational Policy*, 24(1): 23–37.

Grek demonstrates how PISA contributes to national education policy-making. What arguments are put forward to support this view?

The OECD engages in educational standard setting in what is known as 'educational multilateralism' (Mundy, 1998). Standard setting in education is thus elevated beyond the nation-state and, as Resnik (2006) shows, member governments of the OECD increasingly view the relationship between education and the economy in new ways. From a neo-Marxist perspective these multilateral organizations are viewed as 'instruments of Western neoimperialism' (Mundy, 1998: 449) in the global spread of educational policies and practices. Hurst's (1981) analysis unpacks the contradictions and conflicts associated with multi-lateralism as understood by neo-Marxists as well as those taking a more liberal perspective. A neo-Marxist interpretation surrounds power, knowledge and wealth whereby '"aid" is used by the rich to pacify or exploit the poor' (Hurst, 1981: 120). Thus, neo-Marxists would argue there is gain by some and loss by others. A liberal perspective, however, would emphasize the social welfare foundations of these international organizations, including the United Nations Children's Fund (UNICEF), so that poorer nations can become wealthier without impairing the rich. Thus, the liberal view regards aid as the vehicle by which the rich utilize their wealth and knowledge to assist the poor and ignorant.

A key issue for this chapter therefore is unravelling to what extent globalization and/or global factors affect, influence and shape national education policies and the consequences for national education systems. In order to do so the notions of policy-borrowing and policy-learning are explored.

'Policy-borrowing' and 'policy-learning'

From the 1980s onwards greater emphasis has been given to economic competitiveness by nation-states worldwide. Governments, most notably those of Westernized countries, have simultaneously prioritized national economic needs and aligned the aims of their education system with the perceived needs of their country's economy and in relation to the development of human capital (see Chapter 6). The New Public Management (NPM) (Hood, 1995; Ferlie et al., 1996) emerged in the public services of the Westernized world as an organizing mechanism as governments pursued and continued to strive for enhanced efficiency, quality and performance in order to become more economically competitive in the global marketplace. 'New' managerialism emerged due to an increased concern with service quality and measurable outcomes (Pollitt, 1993; Zifcak, 1994) as did a culture of 'performativity'; these global phenomena (Yeatman, 1994) have infiltrated and saturated societies. As a direct consequence, national governments have actively restructured their education systems in the pursuit of greater efficiency and effectiveness, often identifying what they perceive to be similar weaknesses in their systems and similar sets of problems (Halpin and Troyna, 1995). As a means of improving their own provision of education, national governments may look beyond their own system and towards educational ideas and 'policy solutions' in operation elsewhere. This kind of activity has duly accelerated the trend of cross-national education policy-borrowing (Halpin and Troyna, 1995). However, policy-borrowing of this kind is not a recent phenomenon. For example, a reading of the parliamentary debates leading up to the 1870 Elementary Education Act provides evidence of UK policy-makers looking towards the education systems of Germany and the United States of America, for example, for policy ambitions (Hansard, 1870).

Phillips (2011) examines the nature of policy-borrowing in terms of the process of educational transfer between nations arguing that this can take different forms and, as such, postulates a 'spectrum of educational transfer'. This is a five point spectrum ranging from 'Imposed', which Phillips identifies as the totalitarian or authoritarian 'post-conflict occupation of or political domination of one country by another', through to 'Introduced through Influence', a general influence of educational ideas and methods (Phillips, 2011: 4). It is this latter element of the spectrum along with the penultimate element, 'Borrowed Purposefully' signifying the 'intentional copying of policy/practice observed elsewhere' (Phillips, 2011: 4), which is of particular relevance to this chapter. Particular 'cases' that provide different examples of purposeful borrowing will now be examined in turn.

Cases of purposeful policy-borrowing

Dale and Ozga (1993) undertook a comparative study of the impact of 1980s education reform in New Zealand and in England and Wales. They point out that New Right thinking (see Chapter 1) influenced the decision-making in policy at the time; in other words, there is some ideological similarity underpinning the policies of these nations. This can be seen, for example, in the measures taken in New Zealand and in England and Wales to devolve more power to schools (decentralization) and facilitate greater consumer choice. However, the respective policies exhibit clear differences since policies in England and Wales display a tendency towards both the neo-liberal and neo-conservative strands of

New Right thinking. This is evidenced in particular policies stemming from the 1988 ERA for England and Wales such as Local Management of Schools (LMS), which resonates with the neo-liberal strand, and the National Curriculum that has its roots in neo-conservatism. However, in New Zealand, there is less emphasis on neo-conservatism that 'played little, if any, part' (Dale and Ozga, 1993: 85) and more attention given to 'the role of the state and of public administration, informed by particular strands of neo-liberal thought' (ibid.). Thus, while New Right ideology might be considered a general influencing force here, and which was advanced by globalizing tendencies, it must be recognized that there are differential effects that are mediated through national (and local) contexts and cultures in what Ball (1993) regards as 'localised complexity'. The way in which a particular influence might be received at the national level can therefore create a significant divergence of policy.

In contrast to the previous case, David (1993) discusses policy convergence between the United States of America and British school systems and illustrates the clear parallels between the countries in the 1980s; the United States of America and Britain suffered from common economic weaknesses and lacked competitiveness in world markets. Both countries recognized the need for a better-skilled and educated workforce while embracing the neo-liberal tenets of marketization and identifying similar flaws in their school systems such as weak organizational structures and insufficiently accountable 'trendy' teachers (see Chapter 4). David (1993) also points out that successive United States of America administrations and British Governments acknowledged and addressed these limitations in their education systems in comparable ways through a combination of deregulation on the one hand and greater central prescription on the other. Both governments shared an analogous 'crisis' in education, a similar view of the state's role in improving education and policy solutions that fell under the umbrella of 'choice' and diversity (Edwards and Whitty, 1992). Examples of education policy convergence can be seen in the early 1990s between the magnet schools of the United States of America and the privately sponsored CTCs in the United Kingdom (Walford, 2000). Also, there are similarities between the Grant-maintained Schools in England, schools that opted out of LEA control and finance following the 1988 ERA, and the emergence of US charter schools that followed in the early 1990s (Wohlstetter and Anderson, 1994). Occurrences of trans-atlantic policy-borrowing and policy-learning are thus clearly illustrated by these examples.

However, the straightforward parallels within education policy between the United States of America and Britain being presented here can be somewhat misleading; a more comprehensive analysis of this particular case reveals areas of policy divergence. Halpin and Troyna (1995), for example, note that, as in the case of New Zealand, the USA policies have more of a neo-liberal than neo-conservative emphasis. They maintain the reforms of the 1980s in the United States of America around school choice as well as being a New Right ideal were promoted by the Liberal Left to accentuate parental involvement as well as redress historical educational disadvantage. This is quite different from Britain where the sway of the political Right essentially brought about a consolidation of fundamental inequalities of educational opportunity and social inequity through its parental choice policies (Gewirtz, et al., 1995) (see Chapter 3). Also, neo-conservatism is more apparent in the United Kingdom where successive Conservative Governments took steps to prescribe a mandated National Curriculum and weaken the control of LEAs in order to standardize and centralize control over education. Conversely, the control of education in the United States of America lies at the state level with the local, federal government having much greater involvement in decision-making and very little change driven from the centre. Thus, there is likely to be diversity between states in the United States of America.

Another case from the late 1980s onwards can be made between the Core Curriculum of Norway and the National Curriculum in England (Payne, 2002). The curricula developed differently in spite of a similar adherence by both governments to the global policy discourse around a high-skills economy; both attempted to restructure their education and training systems to this end. For teachers in England this resulted in micro-management: a loss of autonomy, their reduction to the status of 'technicians' who deliver an externally devised curriculum and monitoring by OfSTED to ensure the proper delivery of the curriculum in schools. However, the national context for education in England has been one of a low trust approach to education (Ball, 1994) following the development of highly standardized curricula (in 1988), greater emphasis of basic skills and increasingly standardized forms of assessment that intensified after 1997 (see Chapter 4). Teachers in England thus work in a low flexibility-low trust environment. In Norway, however, teachers are empowered as 'active' professional participants who, unlike their counterparts in England, have been able to engage more in the reform process and shape the curriculum in accordance to local needs. Norway has no schools' inspectorate regime and, in comparison to England, teachers work in a high flexibility-high trust environment (Broadhead, 2001). What this case demonstrates is that while there is global convergence in rhetoric, in reality the response is not necessarily going to be uniform. Different geographical, political, economic, social and cultural contexts again come into play, but what is also evident here is the fundamental conception of the purposes of education in terms of the design of the curriculum. Payne (2002: 134) suggests that there are different conceptions 'of what it means to create a skilled "worker-citizen"'; the English model encompasses 'economising education' and is instrumentalist in nature, while the Norwegian model is based on the notion of 'education for work, democracy and life'.

A further illustrative case is the introduction by the former New Labour Government of Threshold Assessment. This is a form of performance-related pay that was introduced for school teachers in England and Wales in the late 1990s (DfEE, 1999b; 1999c). This form of remuneration restructured the pay scales of teachers in England and Wales as movement through the main pay scale and onto an upper pay scale (post-threshold) became dependent upon performance. Thus, there is a much greater emphasis on performativity in schools (Forrester, 2005). Threshold standards to measure effective performance were developed by the management consultants Hay McBer (DfEE, 2000a). These relate to teachers on the main professional grade and formed part of the professional competence framework of National Standards[1] already devised for the teaching profession (TTA, 1997; 1998a; 1998b). Threshold Assessment was eventually embedded into a system of performance management, which was introduced into all state-maintained schools in England and Wales in 2000 (DfEE, 2000b). Performance management is, in essence, a strategic managerial tool that originates from the private sector although it has been drawn on by the public sector as an audit mechanism for monitoring and measuring with the aim of improving public services. Since the 1980s governments in the United Kingdom and other parts of the Westernized world – namely Australia, New Zealand and the United States of America – have adopted performance management as a mechanism to rectify inadequacies of their public sectors. Performance management was thus presented to teachers in England and Wales as 'the kind of system which is the norm across the public and private sectors' (Blunkett, 1999). There was seemingly no recognition by policy-makers, however, of the limitations of performance management (Forrester, 2011).

Threshold Assessment was introduced by New Labour for a number of reasons, purportedly to 'modernize' the profession (DfEE, 1998a), but also to address problems in the morale, recruitment and retention of teachers. These issues are not unique to the United Kingdom, but have been experienced in education systems around the world where significant policy pressure has been directed towards greater accountability of teachers as a means of improving teaching quality and student outcomes. Mahony et al.'s (2002: 160) comparative study of England and Australia is just one that illustrates the similarities in the nature of these particular 'problems' and policy approaches. Their findings however exemplify the different approaches taken by governments citing the 'complex relationships between the Federal Government and the states' as a fundamental reason for the different policy-making contexts like the example of the federal level of government in Australia resonating with that of the United States of America already provided above. The confines of a chapter limit a fuller discussion here of the complexities of the English model of performance management, but taking the issue of 'standards' alone provides an enlightening illustration of policy convergence/ divergence. 'Effective' teaching has been conceptualized in England and Wales through a set of professional standards. Arguably, all of these standards require a great deal of monitoring. Teachers are required to demonstrate that these standards have been met and thus they place a form of control over teachers' work. Mahony et al. (ibid.: 161) found the use of a '"common" language of educational policy' and 'vocabularies of accountability' in their comparative study. So 'standards' is used conventionally in both. The nature of 'standards' in Australia, however, is understood as teachers monitoring themselves for purposes associated with their own personal developmental needs; hence a completely different emphasis to the way in which 'standards' are comprehended in the United Kingdom. Mahony et al. (ibid.: 162) conclude:

> This is an instance where identical language means very different things. Alternatively language and discourse may proclaim distance from, and indeed rejection of, a particular policy trend whilst implementing very similar procedures under different guises.

Australian participants in Mahony et al.'s (ibid.: 162) study explained the 'occupational impossibility' of implementing the English model of performance management and threshold standards in their context. Nevertheless, the permeation of policy ideas of this nature are promulgated often through the activities of major and influential consultancy firms, such as Hay McBer mentioned above, and also the likes of McKinsey & Company and PricewaterhouseCoopers who are significant and influential international players.

So while Mahony et al.'s (2002) comparative study provides an indication of some homogeneity, there is also evidence of differentiation; it is not the case of 'one-size-fits-all'. While discussing the Australian case here it is interesting to note, as an aside, that the grade of Advanced Skills Teacher (AST), which was incorporated into the education system in England and Wales in 1998, originates from Australia. The AST policy is aimed at attracting and retaining excellent teachers in the classroom, as opposed to them leaving the classroom to take on management duties within their school. ASTs also provide mentoring support for other teachers in their own schools and surrounding locality. The notion of 'expert teacher' is found elsewhere in the world as well, such as in the position of the Highly Accomplished Teacher in United States of America and the Chartered Teacher in Scotland. Again, this demonstrates how international policies share common policy understandings. O'Neill (1995: 9) contends this is 'the new orthodoxy' that represents a shift in the relationship between politics, government and education. The consequences are, as the above cases illustrate, global similarities and local differences.

> **Over to you . . .**
>
> The Conservative/Liberal Democrat Coalition Governments have encouraged interested groups to set up Swedish-style Free Schools. However, evidence suggests that this has increased inequality in Sweden, is expensive and the learning gains are insignificant overall. Read the article by Susanne Wigborg and consider the parallels between the Free School reforms and also the different contexts in which they operate. In your opinion, to what extent is policy-borrowing taking place?
>
> See: Wigborg, S. (2010) 'Learning lessons from the Swedish model', *FORUM*, 52(3): 279–84.

'Policy networks' and 'policy entrepreneurs'

It has been established in this chapter that countries may observe other educational systems to see 'what works' elsewhere and may sometimes 'borrow' particular aspects of policy and practice either purposefully and intentionally or through their general influence and permeation (Phillips, 2011). However, it is quite difficult to fathom just how the process of observing or establishing what works in one place and the ultimate decision to borrow policy actually takes place in reality. It is not necessarily a smooth and straightforward transfer of ideas from one place to another and invariably involves a network of people who mediate policy in some way. Typically, the people in the network may be disparate and unknown to each other as their involvement and participation in the process may not be explicit or directly connected; they could be operating in different ways and even with a different set of not necessarily connected agendas. Nevertheless, what their involvement brings to the process, along with their unique set of knowledge, experiences, contacts, motivations and so on, could serve to influence the development of policy in a particular way. As such, it is quite tricky to disentangle the kind of activity and uncover the relationships within networks in order to comprehend exactly what is involved in the making of policy. As has been discussed earlier in this chapter, motivations for countries being attracted to the educational approaches and methods of others can differ considerably. What is a most fascinating area to research, but is often a very difficult, almost impossible endeavour, is to try and uncover who is actually involved in the observing and facilitation of policy-borrowing, policy-learning and policy-making and how this actually takes place. So, for example, it might be that, aware of a particularly effective or successful development in education, politicians and/ or policy-makers and/or educational practitioners and/or academics make a scheduled international visit elsewhere. This may be with the deliberate intention of witnessing that development in action as it may be being considered as a potential remedy to a particular national policy 'problem'. Or it could be that similar ideas are fermenting at different national levels, but the success of a particular policy in one country provides sufficient evidence for mutual endorsement from ministers or policy-makers in another to implement the policy in their own country. Deeper analysis of these kinds of scenarios uncovers a level of activity that is often invisible and so usually difficult to attribute.

Drawing on the case of the creation of the National College for School Leadership (NCSL)[2] in England the intention here is to provide a clearer insight into the somewhat murky waters of policy-making, which often obscures its complexities, and reveal ways in which policy might be shaped and enacted. The decision by the former New Labour Government to establish the NCSL was initially fuelled by policy-makers' desire to improve school leadership in England. Improving the quality of school leadership was seen by policy-makers in the late 1990s as the solution to a number of 'perceived' problems in education and, the argument went that, improving the quality of leadership would ultimately raise standards in schools. The prevailing discourse was that 'effective' school leadership could not be left to 'chance', but required regulated training and the meeting of national standards (Gunter and Forrester, 2008a). Evidence for the setting up of a National College came from home and, significantly, for purposes of this chapter, from abroad. The Harvard Principal Centre in United States of America, for example, was regarded as a model of good practice and caught the attention of some of those indirectly involved in influencing the decision to create the NCSL. Additionally, the New Labour Government sought advice and assistance from particular educational 'experts' based in United

States of America, Australia and Canada. Gunter and Forrester's (2009: 496) findings illuminate the interplay between 'a range of agents who are actively and variously involved in the development and enactment of policy'. The label of 'agent' is used explicitly to signify a catalytic role involving mediation, facilitation and/or negotiation. Gunter and Forrester (2008b) examined the aims and strategies of New Labour's policy-making specifically in relation to its policies for school leaders and school leadership. They identified a complex set of contributing factors, which ultimately led to the decision to create the NCSL. Interviews with 28 ministers, civil servants, policy advisors and private consultants, who were directly involved in the construction and implementation of this decision, uncovered a 'school leadership policy network' (Gunter and Forrester, 2008a: 144). Significantly, the research revealed aspects of the policy-making process that are hardly ever discussed or written about. As a means of illustrating an area of activity that is not usually made public, the comments of a consultant are presented below. This particular consultant, who operated internationally, spoke about 'facilitating' the policy-making process. This consultant, arguably an individual carrier of policy, divulged the nature of their 'connecting' and 'networking' activities as a consultant advisor:

> Brokers is the most recent expression around this sort of stuff; boundary riders. I don't think it's a set of roles that has been explored, perhaps as much as it might, but part of the reason is because it's not a set of activities that are always well understood, because by definition, 'success' means that it's less visible, deliberately so. It is highly tactical, so therefore it's of a different order. And, to be at the sharp end of it, it practises some arts that are not ones that people necessarily want to reveal. Right. So it's a funny game to be in. (Gunter and Forrester, 2008a: 155)

The extract above illustrates the more subtle and enigmatic roles within the processes of policy-making, policy-learning and policy-borrowing. Gunter and Forrester (2008a; 2008b) ascertained the networks and/ or constructed networks and inter-connections between the various 'policy entrepreneurs' who played a key role in the development and establishment of the NCSL. The activities and involvement of some people involved were sometimes intentional, categorical and forthright; the activities and involvement of others, however, were sometimes more subtle, inadvertent and fortuitous. Nevertheless, the policy entrepreneurs who made up this particular network (nationally and internationally) revealed their 'harmonized dispositions regarding neo-liberal reforms' (Gunter and Forrester, 2009: 354). Their assorted roles and positions, ideas, experiences, strategies and personal connections (i.e. people and organizations who they themselves were connected to nationally and internationally) helped to influence, shape and adapt this policy in a particular way.

Another strand of the same project provides further insight into a particular feature of policy influences and involved interviews with 63 academics[3] (Gunter and Forrester, 2008b). Some have been identified as 'experts' by policy-makers and their advice and opinions officially sought by national government, and by international governments in some cases, on issues relating to school leadership as well as a range of other education-related matters. These particular academics are revered by UK policy-makers as 'legitimate knowers' (Gunter and Forrester, 2010: 56) and who are invited, periodically or through a secondment, into the Department, the National College or to various Select Committees, for example. Some also engage at the international level, working in an advisory capacity for other governments across the globe and/or with multi-lateral organizations, notably the OECD, UNESCO and UNICEF. As such, they are in a position to utilize their 'expert' position via a range of advisory activities that may influence national and international education policies in some way. An academic explained their individual situation:

> I try to position myself as somebody who works within policy and tries to influence it by, at times, offering a critique, but a critique which tries to stay within the environment where you can actually be talking to the people who are making policy and implementing policy. So that's the dangerous collaborating game that I'm involved in, in a way, because inevitably it requires compromises. [. . .] my argument would be that if I took an extreme view of whatever policy it is [. . .] then I know the policy-makers won't even invite me to the discussion. [. . .] Now I think people like myself and others who work with me; by and large we get invited. And then we try to work out how can we influence a thing to achieve the kind of things that we are committed with [. . .] the downside of being inside is that you can collude. And indeed you can be used. [. . .] It's a risky game. (Forrester and Gunter, 2009: 13)

Academic 'experts' thus may also contribute to the development of policy ideas. As the extract from the academic above demonstrates, there is a game to be played and personal motivations may include utilizing their 'expert' position to affect their core educational purpose(s); they influence education policy via advisory activities in a significant way in order to bring about the kind of changes they believe to be required.

The case of the creation of the NCSL thus serves to illustrate the workings of an intertwined web of international and national influences and individuals, which culminated in the inimitable making and implementation of policy. Significantly, the establishment of the NCSL in England sparked a great deal of interest overseas with delegations of inquisitive international observers coming over to Nottingham to visit the College. Equally important, policy-makers from around the globe looking for solutions to their own perceived problems in education watched closely to see what was happening in England. The NCSL was established by policy-makers in response to, and as an antidote for, a particular set of 'perceived' problems in the English education system. A decade or so on, the NCSL promotes itself on its website as a 'unique' college 'dedicated' to the professional development of school leaders and its work as a national and international 'benchmark for excellence in leadership development'. Its website houses a multitude of publications regarding 'up-to-date research on current practice'. Increasingly, the NCSL acts in a consultancy capacity to advise international governments on strategic approaches to school leadership and is prominent in influencing the thinking and practice of school leadership globally. It also collaborates with major consultancy firms, for example, McKinsey & Company and PricewaterhouseCoopers.

To what extent international governments utilize and adopt the thinking and practice billowing from the NCSL in their own systems is, of course, likely to vary and, as has been illustrated above, these will be typically mediated through individual local contexts and cultures. The case of the NCSL however, demonstrates how the outcome of one national policy can have far-reaching implications globally. Policy-borrowing and learning is not a straightforward activity, and all kinds of agendas may be at play, which impact upon and reconcile the making of policy. It is not the case of the 'smooth highway' and an easy transfer of policy from one context to another. For as Dale suggests:

> . . . globalization cannot be reduced to the identical imposition of the same policy on all countries. (Dale, 1999: 2)

The penetrating influences of globalization and global processes discussed at the beginning of this chapter, however, cannot be overlooked, for education policy-learning and borrowing sits within the broader framework of global economic restructuring, global competition, political uncertainties and social change. The chapter has shown how globalization is an inexact term with shifting definitions. It is not a linear, consistent or homogenous process, though it is extremely complex and there are different theories of globalization within the literature. Nevertheless, an appreciation of the effects of globalization enables us to more fully understand education systems and their relationship to society as a whole. Globalization affects national education systems, as has been seen from the case illustrations provided; there is an intersection between global politics and the national education policy-making. Henry et al. (2008: 58) note:

> The political, cultural and economic configurations of globalisation do not deny a space for national policy making – far from it – but they have certainly altered the setting within which national governments establish their policy priorities. They have added new layers to the processes of policy production.

There are global similarities in terms of policy problems and solutions, and so instances of convergence can sometimes be seen. Supranational agencies and international consultancy firms, strongly committed to neo-liberal ideologies and educational priorities, are ardent advocates of the market logic and performance indicators in education. These agencies, along with consultants, academics, experts and researchers, play a significant part in influencing and fuelling a 'global policy paradigm' (Ball, 1999: 199) that legitimates the convergence of economic and educational functions in a global context. However, their capacity to enforce policy direction and decisions should not be overestimated for while there are developments and reforms in education systems, which are connected to the effects of globalization, there are local differences and points of resistance, which lead to divergence. Policy-makers are also operating within similar frames of reference and while there may appear to be parallel policies between nations it is not always the case that one has simply borrowed from the other. Thus, the 'lending' and 'borrowing' of policy, along with the 'teaching of' and 'learning from' policy, can be a very complex process to unravel.

Notes

1 National standards for the teaching profession are in place at entry to the profession (Qualified Teacher Status and Induction), movement through the performance threshold for main scale teachers and for leadership positions (Advanced Skills Teacher and head teachers).
2 The National College for School Leadership was opened in Nottingham in 2000. It was set up to provide a range of accredited training opportunities for head teachers and teachers with leadership roles and also identify, fund and promote leadership-related research. The College building cost £28 million (NCSL, 2002).
3 These were mostly Professors of Education who work, or have previously worked, in various UK universities and, through their research and scholarly activities, were involved in the creation of knowledge about educational/school leadership.

Further reading

Ball, S.J., Goodson, I.F. and Maguire, M. (eds) (2007) *Education, Globalisation and New Times,* Abingdon, Oxon: Routledge.

Burbules, N. and Torres, C. (eds) (2000) *Globalisation and Education: Critical Perspectives,* London: Routledge.

Lauder, H., Brown, P., Dillabough, J.A. and Halsey, A.H. (eds) (2006) *Education, Globalization and Social Change,* Oxford: Oxford University Press.

Lingard, B. and Ozga, J. (eds) (2007) *The RoutledgeFalmer Reader in Education Policy and Politics,* London: Routledge Falmer.

Olssen M., Codd, J.A. and O'Neill, A. (2004) *Education Policy: Globalization, Citizenship and Democracy,* London: Sage.

Rizvi, F. and Lingard, B. (2010) *Globalizing Education Policy,* Abingdon, Oxon: Routledge.

Spring, J. (2009) *Globalization of Education – An Introduction,* London: Routledge.

8 Possibilities for Education Policy

Chapter Outline

Unravelling policy

The title of this book *Education Policy Unravelled* is an interesting one for it can be read as signifying several different things simultaneously. One meaning implies that at heart its purpose is to undo, take apart or disassemble education policy in order to reveal important features and characteristics about content and political formation. Another is that, to the best of our ability, we have endeavoured to provide a lens, or set of theoretical lenses, to make clear the often complex trajectories and inter-relationships between policy and practice, to illuminate important perspectives and further appreciate the nuances of policy-making over time. A third and equally significant point is that in writing this book we have attempted to separate or disentangle some of the threads that constitute an intricately woven tapestry of themes resting upon broader social, political and economic movements such as neo-liberalism and globalization. In the end, we may have *unravelled* (i.e. come undone) in our attempt to unravel some of the complexities involved in education policy-making, but if we have then it is surely because education policy is constantly evolving, in a continuous flow of change and quickly becoming dated as new initiatives and developments come to the fore.

Futures perspectives

It is thus on the theme of transition and social change that we wish to proceed in this final chapter. Until now, we have dealt with a broad range of substantive issues relating to a variety of policy-making themes, including race, identity and citizenship in the context of education for improvement or control, primary education, social justice, post-compulsory education and the economics of education and globalization. In each case we have attempted to chart the continuity of policy development along neo-liberal lines, taking an historical perspective and moving from New Labour tentatively towards the new Coalition Government, in the process drawing attention to the strong similarities and nuanced disagreements between successive modern governments. The accounts have been largely factual and analytical even if expressed from a keenly critical perspective of policy-making aiming to challenge the status quo. However, we now wish to take our analysis further, by invoking a futures perspective that allows us to project somewhat speculatively beyond the 'here' and 'now' towards a number of possibilities to develop education policy in the future. Such analysis will not be based upon what some have referred to as 'hard futures research' (Leaton Gray, 2006), drawing heavily upon the empiricist tradition of quasi-positivist studies and using hard quantitative data to predict accurately and further forecast the outlook for the future. Neither will we be soliciting or otherwise surveying the opinions of policy-making stakeholders to relate our expectations and possibilities for the future of education policy-making and practice. Rather, we intend to be entirely conjectural but also visionary in a way that aligns with what has been termed 'soft-futures research' (ibid.), where ideas about the future, deriving from empirical data, are often more radical, complex and multiple in nature. In our case, however, 'data' is contained in the discourse of policy texts and discursive practices that ritually impact on educational structures, cultures and potential futures. As Leaton Gray (2006: 144) explains:

> The new futures methodology has grown out of a desire to move debate beyond the superficial and obvious . . . in a new way, taking into account the social environments of the researcher as well as the subject. In the case of educational research, this is very important. Deciding who is privileged in any construction of knowledge allows us to see who is making

> assumptions about right and wrong . . . Good citizens are seen to be
> those who appear to understand why government policy is necessary and
> who respond by changing themselves in order to implement it, either
> directly or indirectly. Bad individuals are silenced within this discourse,
> however. Playing with ideas we might decide that examples of the silences
> might vary.

In the spirit of seeking new possibilities and opening up the discourse we
may be regarded 'bad' but fully embrace the term in the interest of
showing alternative pathways and trajectories for future policy-making.
Conceptually, this plays to the idea of 'undoing' perspectives on education
policy but in a way that resists simple reconciliation. Ambiguities and
tensions abound in the various threads of policy we have identified
throughout and are, indeed, important aspects we would wish to retain,
or at least avoid ironing out. For us, such tensions convey dissonance and
dissensus rather than broad agreement, suggesting further that there can
be no philosophical resolution to the question of how best policy can be
formed in the context of the areas we have analysed. This means that
imaginative leaps of speculative new ideas while in one sense improbable,
and possibly far-fetched, can usefully serve to disturb and dislocate
contemporary policy. In this, we produce a more radical critique of the
assumptions underpinning its social and political structures and institutional functioning. We turn now to consider the political context in
which we rehearse an alternative model of social justice through Amartya
Sen's capabilities approach, before considering a range of more radical
possibilities for a futures perspective on education policy, drawing on the
work of Steiner, Neill, Dewey, Illich and Freire.

Political context

A recurring theme throughout the book is the spectre of neo-liberalism,
a modern regime infiltrating education policy at every conceivable level
since the early 1970s, gathering momentum during the 1980s and resur-
facing through the reign of New Labour and into the Coalition settlement.
Successive modern governments have placed a premium on the health
of the domestic economy and its ability to compete internationally in a
fiercely intense global market. Rightly or wrongly, probably since the

mid-1970s, following James Callaghan's speech at Ruskin College Oxford, education has been publicly framed as a panacea for the ills of the economy, and further regarded an important mechanism through which competitive advantage is gained as a means to secure future prosperity. However, this has come at a price the opportunity cost of which is arguably human development. Unfettered instrumentalism has transformed the process of education into a capitalist mode of production from which *human* commodities emerge through the acquisition and application of human capital. Human capital theory dating back to the mid-1960s (Becker, 1964) conveys the idea that human knowledge and skills rather than physical machinery or technological advancement will provide the necessary competitive edge in a powerful, economically driven knowledge economy. We need only reflect upon Chapter 6 and the current state of higher education to realize that the discourse of widening participation is often 'only concerned with the "desire to participate" and universities' recruitment strategies, rather than addressing the "ability to participate", once at university' (Crozier et al., 2010: 168). Again, this serves to reinforce the primacy of economics in the education policy-making equation, a formula through which various forms of measurement and audited credentials translate ultimately into human capital. However, an important question for us to consider is whether education policy-making should continue along this path or whether instead there is a contrasting vision of 'educational quality' that might otherwise lead to more desirable educational outcomes through 'ethical goal revision' (Walker M., 2008)?

Social justice revisited

In Chapter 3, for example, we considered the theme of social justice in a variety of forms and different manifestations, including liberal-humanist, market individualistic and social democratic perspectives. The liberal humanist and social democratic perspectives, in particular, convey a notion of justice along egalitarian lines, but still do not challenge the status quo as they variously attempt to find ways of creating policies and interventions to facilitate improved access, or remove barriers and/or produce new opportunities for disadvantaged groups. The purpose of distributive justice is a redistribution of resources or welfare to enhance or equalize opportunity and participation in the 'weak' sense or, alternatively, to equalize outcomes in the 'stronger' sense. What it does not do more fundamentally, however, is question the framework within which improved opportunities or outcomes are established in order to consider 'difference', and the particular freedoms that individuals have reasons to value.

This kind of theorizing has often been applied historically through the primary curriculum, where in Chapter 4 we noted a gradual and progressive centralization and colonization of primary education from the early 1970s onwards. In a climate of unprecedented reform, notions of social justice still prevailed but the introduction of a more disciplined structure to the curriculum, more heavily prescribed teaching styles and classroom pedagogy and a more clearly defined notion of pupil progress monitored through standardized assessment conspired to reduce choice all round. The National Curriculum was the centrepiece of the ERA (1988) which imposed, in turn, a severe restriction on what could be taught in schools and, more crucially, provided a definitive view on what counts as knowledge. In the spirit of a futures perspective we now ask what primary education might look like if such bureaucratically inspired and centrally driven restrictions were lifted, and if the voice of the younger generation was heard rather than muted, and their ideas usefully acted upon. Our starting point for this debate is the work of economist and political philosopher Amartya Sen.

Sen's perspective on social justice is markedly different from all others, for his concept of equality of capability, articulated through a 'capabilities' approach to social justice, is based on the notion of opportunity freedoms, which place emphasis on the 'functionings' of individuals to 'be' and 'do': 'to choose the lives they have reasons to value. It is this actual freedom that is represented by the person's "capability" to achieve various alternative combinations of functionings' (Sen, 1992: 81). Put simply, this means that individuals are to be regarded as 'ends' in themselves, rather than as 'means' to other social and political ends, as noted, for example, in Chapter 5 on post-compulsory education, where vocational education's overt policy aim is economic growth. This represents an interesting political shift because if individuals are to live not just free from constraint but with the possibility of acting upon real choices (what Berlin [1969] would call 'positive liberty'), then policy and process in education are likely to necessitate some reconfiguration and 'ethical goal revision' (Walker M., 2008). In this revised context, then, educational processes would be required to countenance an evaluation of the conditions that individuals need in order to thrive and further enable their potential to be realized.

Five alternative philosophies

The suggestion for primary education is to dispense with the model of a formal National Curriculum in order to adopt a more nuanced and progressive approach to education in children's formative years. The Steiner model ([1907] 1996) offers an alternative ideology, encouraging a unity of the mind, body and soul, and which is free from the shackles of the state and imposition of a centrally prescribed curriculum. However, even with such apparent extended freedoms (from constraint), there are significant limitations imposed through the particular requirements of a spiritual dimension. Accordingly, Steiner is neither child-centred nor freedom-based, but instead imposes a discipline through a structured curriculum and daily routine or rhythm related to the teaching of spirituality. In this crucial respect it parts company with the concept of a capabilities approach as advocated by Sen.

A different alternative model in the recent history of contemporary education, and one that departs radically from mainstream policy is the democratic philosophy and practice of the Summerhill School. Founded by A.S. Neill in 1924, the Summerhill School focuses on securing the emotions of young people and their contentment both at school and across the life course. As Neill (1968: 20; 99) explains:

> We set out to make a school in which we should allow children to be themselves. In order to do this we had to renounce all discipline, all direction, all suggestion, all moral training, all religious instruction . . . If the emotions are permitted to be really free, the intellect will look after itself.

We believe the democratic model of Summerhill has a great deal in common with Sen's capabilities approach, not least the emphasis placed upon individuals having particular freedoms to orient themselves around the things they have reasons to value. This offers the potential for what Neill refers to as 'inner contentment' and personal fulfilment. Moreover, the democratic ethos of Summerhill is a fundamental element of institutional and cultural life within the school, as exemplified through the 'Meeting' that takes place three, or possibly four, times per week and is held mainly in order 'to scrutinise breaches of the democratically agreed Laws' (Garratt and Piper, 2012: in press). In this, pupil voice is more than a rhetorical device; it is an essential characteristic of life within the school. However, since 'Summerhill School operates as a closed community' (ibid.) we suggest that while in one sense it provides a propitious example of positive liberty it does little to bridge the gap between the individual and the social, young people and their local communities. It is our contention that the future of education policy should not be concerned exclusively with individual learning but should also nurture an ethical social disposition, as part of the ambit of living within an inclusive learning society.

To this end, we call upon a third example and the work of John Dewey ([1916] 2007) in *Democracy and Education*. For Dewey, school and community are not separate entities but rather different sides of the same coin of democracy, insofar as a democratic school is regarded the best preparation for a democratic society. Dewey also suggests that personal growth does not occur from what is already there but rather through a gradual expansion of experience according to the social and cultural environment into which young people are socialized. This means that learning amounts to more than a facile gathering of facts or simple acquisition of propositional knowledge; it is rather more concerned with experience and philosophical enquiry that provides important edification for ideas, meanings and values allowing the possibility for young people to develop socially and educationally. So, while 'thinking is as much an individual matter as is the digestion of food' (ibid.: 223), such activity is socially and culturally embedded, for 'when the social factor is absent, learning becomes a carrying over of some presented material into a purely individual consciousness' (ibid.: 222). Importantly, Dewey considers that the relegation of social interests to a traditionally academic curriculum is likely to produce a 'rupture of social continuity' (ibid.: 238) and further forge a separation of 'practical and intellectual activity, man and nature, individuality and association, culture and vocation', culminating in the separation of, 'knowing and doing, theory and practice, between mind as the end and spirit of action and the body as its organ and means' (ibid.: 246). While the social dimension of education is undoubtedly important for Dewey, much like Sen his conception of learning is that it be structured around the interests of young people through what he calls the 'instrument of effective self-direction' or learning by *doing*. This determination to avoid blueprints in learning does not, however, eclipse the crucial role of the teacher in the educational process, in helping children link their interests to sustained intellectual development and educative experiences. For us, a point of contention is what can be seen to count here as an educative experience and to what extent teachers may become involved in the process of determining what counts as knowledge; that is what is considered legitimate and, alternatively, what is not.

Going still further, a fourth alternative example providing a more radical means to address the problem of closed communities and teacher indoctrination is advanced through the work of Ivan Illich (1971). In his book *Deschooling Society* Illich assembles a compelling critique of the corrupting impact of institutions (i.e. schools) on young people, in particular their tendency to institutionalize myths about society. One such widely propagated 'myth' is that the 'imagination is "schooled" to accept service in place of value' (Illich, 1971: 9). As he elaborates further:

> Equal educational opportunity is . . . both a desirable and a feasible goal, but to equate this with obligatory schooling is to confuse salvation with the Church. School has become the world religion of a modernized prole-tariat, and makes futile promises of salvation to the poor of the techno-logical age . . . neither learning nor justice is promoted by schooling because educators insist on packaging instruction with certification. (Illich, 1971: 10–11)

This critique resonates strongly against the perspective presented in Chapters 5, 6 and 7, in which we conveyed the impact of the neo-liberal regime upon contemporary policy and politics, and neat alignment with instrumental education and training. For Illich, the concept of learning is often confused and conflated with teaching, which carries with it ulterior motives and purposes. A relatively recent example of this is the development of the so-called free-school movement, not to be confused with iconic historical examples like Summerhill, the Scotland Road Free School in Liverpool or the White Lion School in London, which are/ were affirmed on democratic principles and freedom-based education of a libertarian ilk. Rather, the new political movement of free-schools, a programme receiving £130 million of government investment for 24 new start-ups in the autumn of 2011, is reported by some as flattering to deceive. As Benn (2011) argues:

> Few among this first wave are truly parent-promoted projects, and nor are they likely to benefit the most deprived in our society. Instead this is an odd, hybrid movement that incorporates failing independent schools, diverse faith groups, and charitable educational groups . . . the final irony may be that parents flood back to local schools as the increasingly unattractive values of niche marketing, social snobbery and religious interests begin to take hold. Broad-based secular comprehensives that draw in families across the class, faith and ethnic spectrum, entirely free of private control, could hold a new appeal.

This resonates strongly with Illich's point that if we can deinstitution-alize education, then we may, in turn, be able to deinstitutionalize society and so dispel myths surrounding the neo-liberal agenda, in particular the trend to impose private interests and agendas (see, for example, Beckett, 2007) upon the educational needs of young people and/or the accumulation of qualifications in pursuit of human capital. Interestingly, Illich's philosophy offers the possibility of reinventing learning in ways that respect the capability freedoms of individuals (vis-à-vis Sen), but which also embraces a social policy dimension in connecting people through 'peer matching' and communication/learning networks, that is where people list the skills they wish to acquire (what Illich calls 'skill exchanges') and find a match to work with, and learn from others in a collaborative fashion. A further dimension to Illich's book proffers that institutionalized education is a luxury good and that public funding should not be used to finance state education. While the current state system is some way off reaching this conclusion, the future of higher education in England is lurching ever nearer to this outcome. Annual student fees of up to £9,000 are reported to be the third highest in the developed world according to a recent OECD study of 34 countries

(Vasagar and Shepherd, 2011), and the government's contribution to higher education in England is some two percentage points lower than the OECD average of 5.9 per cent of Gross Domestic Product (GDP). If this is not serious enough in terms of the implications for social justice and the projected future decline in participation of young people in higher education (Vasagar, 2011), the fact that tuition fees are variable (some might say radically different) across the United Kingdom raises a further question of equity in the process. For example, not only is there some regional variation across universities in England setting fees, for example, Birkbeck University charging a minimum fee of £6,000, the University of West London charging £7,500 and most Russell Group Universities charging the maximum fee of £9,000 in 2012 (in fact all 123 higher education institutions in England will be charging more than £6,000 in 2012), elsewhere in the United Kingdom tuition fees are significantly lower (Sedghi and Shepherd, 2011). The Scottish Government, for example, will be subsidizing tuition fees to the tune of £5,000 for many courses (Kemp, 2011), while all ten Welsh universities have been barred from charging maximum fees, and are more likely to be setting fees at a little more than £4,000 per annum in 2012 (Sedghi and Shepherd, 2011). Aside from the fact this may well encourage young people to seek higher education elsewhere in Europe, for example, at Trinity College in Dublin where no fees apply to UK students, or at Amsterdam University where undergraduate courses are taught in English, but where fees are a fraction of those in England at £1,516 per annum (Bawden, 2011), the fact remains there is a discernible ratcheting-up of fees and reduction in public funding of higher education in England that is limiting the capabilities of disadvantaged students while privileging those from more affluent backgrounds.

Thus, while we agree with the spirit of Illich's former point on deinstitutionalizing state education for appropriate normative reasons, we must part company with his argument that formal education is a luxury good, to be enjoyed (by default) only by a privileged minority, on important ethical grounds. Indeed, a further problem in the process of deinstitutionalizing education is that it has the potential to encourage prejudice and fanaticism among networks of like-minded individuals, to the detriment of the interests of other people and communities within society. Consider, for example, the thorny problem of citizenship education as noted in

Chapter 2 and the historical absence of critical discourses around 'race' and ethnicity in education policy and practice at all levels of engagement. To address this shortfall we suggest education requires a different trajectory that might offer a more discerning critical pedagogy.

One such model can be found in the work of political philosopher Paulo Freire ([1970] 1993) and his seminal book *Pedagogy of the Oppressed*. For Freire, the project of education is not so much to encourage 'social continuity' as with Dewey, but instead a reconstruction of education through social responsibility and the development of critical thinking relating to the conditions of society. In this transformatory project, teachers and students work together to question dominant practices and ideologies so that education always involves social relations and is always essentially a political act. Freire suggests that education can be liberating only if it helps us understand the world we live in:

> the oppressed . . . must perceive the reality of oppression not as a closed world from which there is no exit, but as a limiting situation which they can transform. (ibid.: 31)

In Chapter 2 we discussed the problem of successive policies for citizenship education which had served to erase discourses of 'race' and ethnicity through what some critical race theorists (Gilborn, 2009) call a 'naturalized', 'sanitized' or 'white-washed' version of history and 'majoritarian' conception of 'Britishness'. A more critical orientation, however, would allow the absent presence of 'race' in citizenship discourses to be challenged through a process of 'conscientization' (raising critical awareness in order to promote change) and purposeful 'dialogue' between teachers and students in a reciprocal relationship of co-intentionality. As Freire ([1970] 1993: 53) notes 'education must begin with the solution of the teacher-student contradiction . . . both are simultaneously teachers *and* students'. This would serve to address the problem widely reported in the research literature that many teachers are reluctant to engage with issues of 'race' and 'racism' and so avoid them completely. Or the recently reported problem that far-right political groups, such as the English Defence League, are beginning to fill a vacuum left by mainstream politics and political parties (Meikle, 2011), many of whom are failing to win the hearts and minds of young people in local communities. Through a form of Freirean 'praxis' it is possible to envisage how adults and young people might be brought closer together inter-generationally in order to challenge and subvert traditional hierarchies and further engender greater equity in education, starting with the cultural experiences of young people or their community cultural wealth (Yosso, 2005), as a means to challenge prejudice and potentially harmful extremism.

An additional feature of Freirean praxis, is the critique of education as 'banking', that is the accumulation of facts and information as a political device to obscure critical consciousness and thus preserve the status quo. Revisiting the theme of primary education, for example, it is possible to imagine in this context how the process of learning to read can be taken well beyond the teaching of synthetic phonics, to incorporate a process of political literacy, so that becoming literate is not just learning to read, but developing greater political awareness of the world around us – that is, learning to 'read' the world. This futures perspective, we contend, is apt to nurture not only a more critical disposition in young people but also a more socially just approach to education through enhanced recognition of the internal capabilities of young people (the capacity to realize individual potential) (Nussbaum, 2000).

In a different context we believe that Freirean philosophy may be usefully applied to the instrumental and potentially exploitative situation developing in post-compulsory education. Earlier, in Chapter 5, we noted the popular belief in the ability of school-based education or work-based training to provide the engine for economic growth, and argued that unfettered instrumentalism had created a focus upon human capital and, with this, a preoccupation with 'academic functionings' (or credentials) at the expense of capabilities (personal freedoms). While Sen (1999: p. xi) is correct to point out that 'the freedom of agency that we individually have is inescapably qualified and constrained by the social, political and economic opportunities that are available to us', or in educational terms that 'individuals only have choices . . . to the extent that prevailing structures – of curriculum, pedagogy, and assessment of learning' (Garratt, 2011: 217) are sensitive to 'difference' and the effect of 'social arrangements and social relations upon individual lives' (Walker and Unterhalter, 2007: 10), we believe that Freirean praxis may provide a useful antidote to the hegemony of neo-liberal policy and politics. Thus, rather than vocational education and training setting out to prepare young people for their role in the world of work (and capitalist mode of production), we would encourage the development of improved political literacy in the sense of helping less privileged communities recognize the conditions of their oppression as concealed, for example, in the rhetoric of David Cameron's political speech concerning 'real qualifications' (privileging 'functionings' rather than 'capabilities') at the beginning of Chapter 2.

In our aim to open up the discourse around education policy, anticipating a different and more liberated future, we have invoked several useful perspectives and philosophical trajectories, drawing on the work of Steiner, Neill, Dewey, Illich and Freire. In the spirit of a 'soft-futures' approach that resists stepping 'outside of the discourse in order to find objectivity' (Leaton Gray, 2006: 146), and which refuses to position ideas in a hierarchy, we prefer to accept, and live with complexity and multiplicity. This is reflected in the overlaps (imbrications) and spaces in between (liminality of) the philosophical perspectives considered above, each of which reveal significant possibilities for the future direction of education policy, but none that are definitive or all-encompassing. In our consideration of the future we note the ambivalence and uncertainty that is characteristic of the contradictions and confusions at the heart of policy reform. Our methodological response to the issues raised throughout this book, is to propose a more optimistic construction of ideas from diverse sources (i.e. bricolage) and philosophical possibilities, taking us beyond the current constraints of neo-liberal policy to a more democratic future. Here, critical involvement rather than implicit resolution might usefully create the intellectual conditions to enable individual capabilities to flourish. However, ultimately, only deliberative ethical goal revision is likely to achieve a radical shift in the axis of education policy towards a more socially just and democratic future.

References

Adler, M. E., Petch, A. J. and Tweedie, J. W. (1989) *Parental Choice and Educational Policy.* Edinburgh: Edinburgh University Press.

Alexander, R. (1984) *Primary Teaching.* London: Hold, Rinehart & Winston.

— (2010) 'Implications of the Cambridge Primary Review for primary initial teacher education'. *The Cambridge Primary Review and Initial teacher Education.* Universities' Council for the Education of Teachers (UCET) and National Primary Teacher Education Council (NaPTEC): Manchester, 26 March.

Alexander, R., Rose, J. and Woodhead, C. (1992) *Curriculum, Organisation and Classroom Practice in Primary Schools: A Discussion Paper.* London: HMSO.

Alexander, R. J. (ed.) (2009) *Children, their World, their Education: Final Report and Recommendations of the Cambridge Primary Review.* Abingdon: Routledge.

Angus, L. (1994) 'Sociological analysis and education management: The social context of the self managing school', *British Journal of Sociology of Education.* 15(1): 79–91.

Apple, M. (1999) 'The absent presence of race in educational reform', *Race Ethnicity and Education.* 2(1): 9–16.

Apple, M. W. (1990) *Ideology and Curriculum* (2nd edn). London: Routledge.

Arnot, M., David, M. and Weiner, G. (1999) *Closing the Gender Gap – Postwar Education and Social Change.* Cambridge: Polity Press.

Ball, S. J. (1990) *Politics and Policy Making in Education – Exploration in Policy Sociology.* London: Routledge.

— (1993) 'What is policy? Texts, trajectories and toolboxes', *Discourse.* 13(20): 10–17.

— (1994) *Education Reform: A Critical and Post-structural Approach.* Buckingham: Open University Press.

— (1999) 'Labour, learning and the economy: A "policy sociology" perspective', *Cambridge Journal of Education.* 29(2): 195–206.

— (2007) *Education plc – Understanding Private Sector Participation in Public Sector Education.* London: Routledge.

— (2008) *The Education Debate.* Bristol: Policy Press.

Ball, S. J., Bowe, R. and Gewirtz, S. (1995) 'Circuits of schooling: A sociological exploration of parental choice of school in social class contexts', *Sociological Review.* 43(1): 52–78.

Barber, M. (1992) *Education and the Teacher Unions.* London: Cassell.

Barker, M. (1981) *The New Racism.* London: Junction Books.

Barr, N. (2004) 'Higher Education Funding', *Oxford Review of Economic Policy.* 20(2): 264–83.

Batho, G. (1990) *Political Issues in Education.* London: Cassell.

Bawden, A. (2011) 'World university rankings show that good higher education can be a bargain', *The Guardian*, 5 September, www.guardian.co.uk/education/2011/sep/05/world-university-rankings-low-fees?INTCMP=SRCH, [accessed 23 September 2011].

BBC (2008) 'British citizenship tests planned', *BBC News*, 20 February, http://news.bbc.co.uk/1/hi/uk_politics/7253933.stm, [accessed 31 August 2008].

Beck, U. (2000a) 'The cosmopolitan perspective: Sociology of the second age of modernity', *British Journal of Sociology*. 51(1): 79–105.

— (2000b) *What is Globalization?* Cambridge: Polity Press.

— (2006) *Cosmopolitan Vision*. Cambridge: Polity Press.

Becker, G. (1964) *Human Capital*. Chicago: University of Chicago Press.

— (1993) *Human Capital* (3rd edn). Chicago: University of Chicago Press.

Beckett, F. (2007) *The Great City Academy Fraud*. London: Continuum.

Benn, M. (2011) 'The real cost of "free" schools will be paid by the poorest', *The Guardian*, 8 September, www.guardian.co.uk/commentisfree/2011/sep/08/cost-free-schools-paid-by-poorest, [accessed 23 September 2011].

Bennett, N. (1992) 'Beyond Ruskin: Recent conceptions of children's learning and implications for primary school practice', in M. Williams, R. Daugherty and F. Banks (eds) *Continuing the Education Debate*. London: Cassell (pp. 65–73).

Berlin, I. (1969) *Four Essays on Liberty*. Oxford: Oxford University Press.

Bernstein, B. (1968) 'Education cannot compensate for society', *New Society*. 387: 334–7.

Blair, T. (1996) *New Britain – My Vision of a Young Country*. London: Fourth Estate Ltd.

— (1998) *The Government's Annual Report 1997–98*. London: The Stationary Office.

Blunkett, D. (1998) 'Cash for competence', *Times Educational Supplement*. 24 July, www.tes.co.uk.

— (1999) *New Teachers' Pay Arrangements will cut Through Bureaucracy*, Association of Teachers and Lecturers' Annual Conference, Harrogate, 30 March, DfEE Press Release, 139/99.

Blyth, W. A. L. (1965) *English Primary Education* (Part 2), London: Routledge, Kegan Paul.

Board of Education (1931) *The Primary School*. Consultative Committee Report (The Hadow Report). London: HMSO.

Boden, R. and Nedeva, M. (2010) 'Employing discourse: Universities and graduate "employability"', *Journal of Education Policy*. 25(1): 37–54.

Boffey, D. (2011) 'Willetts in secret talks with banks on funding of student loans', *The Observer*. 26 June: 6.

Bourdieu, P. and Passeron, J. C. (1990) *Reproduction in Education, Society and Culture* (2nd edn), London: Sage.

Boyles, D., Carusi, T. and Attick, D. (2009) 'Historical and critical interpretations of social justice', in W. Ayers, T. Quinn and D. Stovall (eds) *Handbook of Social Justice in Education*. Abingdon, Oxon: Routledge (pp. 30–42).

Braithwaite, R. J. (1992) 'School Choice as a Means of Attaining Excellence in Education', *Cambridge Journal of Education*. 22(1): 43–53.

Broadhead, P. (2001) 'Curriculum change in Norway: Thematic approaches, active learning and pupil cooperation – from curriculum design to classroom implementation', *Scandinavian Journal of Educational Research.* 45(1): 19–36.

Brown, G. (2004) 'The golden thread that runs throughout history', *The Guardian.* 8 July. www.guardian.co.uk/politics/2004/jul/08/britishidentity.economy/print, [accessed 23 July 2009].

— (2006) 'Who do we want to be? The future of Britishness', Speech presented at the Fabian New Year Conference, January 14, Imperial College, London.

Brown, P., Hesketh, A. and Williams, S. (2003) 'Employability in a knowledge-driven economy', *Journal of Education and Work.* 16(2): 107–26.

Brown, P. and Lauder, H. (1996) 'Education, globalization and economic development', *Journal of Education Policy.* 11(1): 1–25.

— (1992) 'Education, economy and society: An introduction to a new agenda', in P. Brown and H. Lauder (eds) *Education for Economic Survival: From Fordism to Post-fordism?* London: Routledge.

Browne, J. (2010) *Securing a Sustainable Future for Higher Education – An Independent Review of Higher Education Funding and Student Finance* (The Browne Report). London: Department for Business, Innovations and Skills.

Bryman, A. (2004) *The Disneyization of Society.* London: Sage.

Burbules, N. C. and Torres, C. A. (2000) 'Globalisation and Education: An Introduction', in N. C. Burbules and C. A. Torres (eds) *Globalisation and Education: Critical Perspectives.* London: Routledge.

Butterfield, S. (1995) *Educational Objectives and National Assessment.* Buckingham: Open University Press.

Cabinet Office (1999) *Modernising Government.* (Cm. 4310). London: The Stationary Office.

— (2010) *The Coalition: Our Programme for Government.* London: Cabinet Office.

— (2011) *Building the Big Society.* London: Cabinet Office.

Central Advisory Council for Education, England (CACE) (1967) *Children and Their Primary Schools: A Report* (The Plowden Report). London: HMSO.

Callaghan, J. (1976) 'Towards a national debate', The Great Debate: 25 years on, *Education Guardian.* 15 October 2001, http://education.guardian.co.uk/thegreatdebate/story/0,, 574645,00.html [accessed 18 April 2011].

Callinicos, A. (2010) *Bonfire of Illusions – The Twin Crises of the Liberal World.* Cambridge: Policy Press.

Campbell, R. J. and Neill, S. R. St. J. (1994) *Primary Teachers at Work.* London: Routledge.

Campbell, R. J. (2001) 'The colonisation of the primary curriculum', in R. Phillips and J. Furlong (eds) *Education Reform and the State – Twenty-five Years of Politics, Policy and Practice.* London: RoutledgeFalmer (pp. 31–44).

Capling, A., Considine, M. and Crozier, M. (1998) *Australian Politics in the Global Era.* Melbourne: Addison-Wesley.

Carr, W. (1991) 'Education for citizenship', *British Journal of Educational Studies.* 39(2): 373–85.

Carroll, S. and Walford, G. (1997) 'Parents' Responses to the School Quasi-market', *Research Papers in Education.* 12(1): 3–26.

Castells, M. (1997) *The Power of Identity: The Information Age: Economy, Society and Culture* (Vol. 1). Oxford: Blackwell.

— (2000) *End of Millennium* (2nd edn). Oxford: Blackwell.

Confederation of British Industry (CBI) (1989) *Towards a Skills Revolution.* London: CBI.

— (1993) *Routes for Success – Careership: A Strategy for All 16–19 Year Old Learners.* London: CBI.

Cerny, P. (1997) 'Paradoxes of the competition state: The dynamics of political globalization', *Government and Opposition.* 32(2): 251–74.

Chapman, C. and Gunter, H. M. (eds) (2009) *Radical Reforms – Perspectives on an Era of Educational Change.* Abingdon, Oxen: Routledge.

Chapman, L. and West-Burnham, J. (2010) *Education for Social Justice – Achieving Wellbeing for All.* London: Continuum.

Chitty, C. (1989) *Towards a New Education System: The Victory of the New Right?* London: Falmer Press.

— (2009) *Education Policy in Britain.* Cambridge: Polity Press.

Clarke, J. and Newman, J. (1997) *The Managerial State – Power, Politics and Ideology in the Remaking of Social Welfare.* London: Sage.

Clemitshaw, G. and Jerome, L. (2009) 'Can citizenship education promote democracy and Britishness? A survey of trainee teachers' attitudes on the purposes of citizenship education', *CitizED Report.* www.citized.info/pdf/commarticles/Citized%20 Britishness%20Professional%20Report%20FINAL%20May09.doc, [accessed 23 July 2009].

Coard, B. (1971) *How the West Indian Child Is Made ESN in the British School System.* London: New Beacon Books.

Coffield, F. (1999) 'Breaking the Consensus: Lifelong learning as social control', *British Educational Research Journal.* 25(4): 479–99.

Considine, M. (1994) *Public Policy: A Critical Approach,* Melbourne. Australia: Macmillan Education.

Coughlan, S. (2010) 'Students face tuition fees rising to £9,000', *BBC News Education and Family.* 3 November 2010, www.bbc.co.uk/news/education-11677862 [accessed 12 May 2011].

Coulby, D. (1989a) 'From educational partnership to central control', in L. Bash and D. Coulby, *The Education Reform Act – Competition and Control.* London: Cassell Educational Ltd.

— (1989b) 'The National Curriculum', in L. Bash and D. Coulby, *The Education Reform Act – Competition and Control,* London: Cassell Educational Ltd.

Cox, C. B. and Boyson, R. (eds) (1975) Black Paper 4, *Fight for Education.* London: Dent.

— (eds) (1977) Black Paper 5, *Black Paper 1977,* March. London: Temple Smith.

Cox, B. and Dyson, A. E. (eds) (1969a) Black Paper 1, *Fight for Education,* March. London: Critical Quarterly Society.

— (eds) (1969b) Black Paper 2, *The Crisis in Education*, October. London: Critical Quarterly Society.

— (eds) (1970) Black Paper 3, *Goodbye Mr. Short*, November. London: Critical Quarterly Society.

Crick, B. (2000) *Essays on Citizenship*. London: Continuum.

Crozier, G., Reay, D. and Clayton, C. (2010) 'The socio-cultural and learning experiences of working-class students in higher education', in M. David (ed.) *Improving Learning by Widening Participation in Higher Education*. London: Routledge (pp. 62–74).

Cunningham, P. (1988) *Curriculum Change in the Primary School Since 1945 – Dissemination of the Progressive Ideal*. London: The Falmer Press.

Curtis, P. (2007) 'UK falls to 14th place in science teaching table', *Education Guardian*, 29 November 2007, www.guardian.co.uk/education/2007/nov/29/schools.uk1?INTCMP=SRCH [accessed 20 May 2011].

Curtis, S. J. (1967) *History of Education in Great Britain* (6th edn). London: University Tutorial Press.

Dadds, M. (1992) 'The changing face of topic work in the primary curriculum', *The Curriculum Journal*. 4(2): 253–67.

Dale, R. (1999) 'Specifying globalization effects on national policy: A focus on the mechanisms', *Journal of Education Policy*. 14(1): 1–17.

Dale, R. and Ozga, J. (1993) 'Two hemispheres – both New Right? 1980's education reform in New Zealand and England and Wales', in R. Lingard, J. Knight and P. Porter (eds) *Schooling Reform in Hard Times*. Lewis: Falmer Press.

David, M. E. (1980) *The State, the Family and Education*. London: Routledge and Kegan Paul.

— (1993) *Parents, Gender and Education Reform*. Cambridge: Polity Press.

— (ed.) (2010) *Improving Learning by Widening Participation in Higher Education*. London: Routledge.

Dearing, R. (1993) *The National Curriculum and its Assessment: Interim Report*. York and London: NCC/SEAC.

— (1996a) *Review of Qualifications for 16–19 Year Olds*. Hayes, Middlesex: SCAA.

— (1996b) *Report of the National Committee of Inquiry into Higher Education*. London: DfEE Publications.

Department for Business Innovation and Skills (BIS) (2011) *Higher Education: Students at the Heart of the System* (Cm. 8122). London: HMSO.

Department of Employment (DE) (1988) *Training for Employment*. London: HMSO.

Department of Employment/ Department of Education and Science (DE/DES) (1986) *Working Together – Education and Training*. London: HMSO.

Deem, R. (2004) 'Sociology and the Sociology of Higher Education – a missed call or a disconnection?' *International Studies in the Sociology of Education*. 14(1): 21–45.

Delanty, G. (2008) 'Academic identities and institutional change', in R. Barnett and R. Di Napoli (eds) *Changing Identities in Higher Education – Voicing Perspectives*. London: Routledge.

Department of Education and Science (DES) (1972) *Education: A Framework for Expansion* (Cm. 5174). London: HMSO.

— (1977) *Education in Schools: A Consultative Document* (Cmnd. 6869). London: HMSO.

— (1978) *Primary Education in England: A Survey by HMI.* London: HMSO.

— (1981) *The School Curriculum.* London: HMSO.

— (1984) *Parental Influence at School: A New Framework for School Government in England and Wales,* Green Paper (Cmnd. 9242). London: HMSO.

— (1985a) *The Curriculum from 5–16: Curriculum Matters 2.* London: HMSO.

— (1985b) *The Development of Higher Education into the 1990s.* London: HMSO.

— (1987a) *Primary Staffing Survey.* London: HMSO.

— (1987b) *Higher Education: Meeting the Challenge* (Cm. 114). London: HMSO.

— (1988) *Advancing A-levels, Report of the Committee Chaired by Professor Higginson.* London: HMSO.

— (1991a) *Education and Training for the 21st Century.* London: HMSO.

— (1991b) *Higher Education: A New Framework* (Cm. 1541). London: HMSO.

Department for Education (DfE) (2011a) *Positive for Youth – Young People's Involvement in Decision Making,* Discussion Paper. London: DfE.

— (2011b) *Timetable for the National Curriculum Review.* Available at: www.education.gov.uk/schools/teachingandlearning/curriculum/nationalcurriculum/a0073092/timetable-for-the-national-curriculum-review, [accessed 12 April 2011].

Department for Education and Employment (DfEE) (1997a) *Excellence in Schools* (Cm. 3681). London: Stationery Office.

— (1997b) *Excellence in Cities.* London, DfEE.

— (1997c) *Qualifying for Success: A Consultation Paper on the Future of Post-16 Qualifications.* London: Crown Copyright.

— (1998a) *Teachers: Meeting the Challenge of Change.* London: The Stationary Office.

— (1998b) National Literacy Strategy Framework for Teaching. London: DfEE.

— (1998c) National Numeracy Framework. London: DfEE.

— (1998d) *The Learning Age: A Renaissance for a New Britain.* London: HMSO.

— (1998e) *Higher Education for the 21st Century – Response to the Dearing Report.* London: DfEE.

— (1999a) *Learning to succeed: a new framework for post-16 learning.* London: DfEE Publications.

— (1999b) *Teachers: Meeting the Challenge of Change – Technical Consultation Document on Pay and Performance Management.* London: DfEE Publications Centre.

— (1999c) *Performance Management Framework for Teachers: Consultation Document.* London: DfEE Publications.

— (2000a) *A Model of Teacher Effectiveness. Report by Hay McBer to the Department for Education and Employment.* London: The Stationary Office.

— (2000b) *Performance Management in Schools. Performance Management Framework.* (Guidance. Teachers and Staffing). London: DfEE Publications. (Ref: DfEE 0051/2000).

Department for Education/Employment Department and Welsh Office (DfE/ED/WO) (1991) *Education and Training for the 21st Century.* London: HMSO.

Department for Education and Skills (DfES) (2003a) *Excellence and Enjoyment. A Strategy for Primary Schools.* London: DfES.

— (2003b) *The Future of Higher Education.* London: HMSO.

— (2004) *Every Child Matters: Change for Children.* London: HMSO.

— (2005) *14–19 Education and Skills.* London: DfES.

— (2007) *Curriculum Review: Diversity and Citizenship* (Ajegbo Report). London: DfES.

Department for Education and Skills, Department of Trade and Industry and Department for Work and Pensions (DfES/DTI/DWP) (2003) *21st Century Skills Realising our Potential: Individuals, Employers, Nation.* London: DfES/DTI/DWP.

Dewey, J. ([1916] 2007) *Democracy and Education.* Teddington, Middlesex: Echo Library.

Docking, J. (2000) 'What is the solution? An overview of national policies for schools, 1979–99', in J. Docking (ed.) *New Labour's Policies for Schools. Raising the Standard.* London: David Fulton Publishers (pp.21–42).

Driver, S. (2008) 'New Labour and social policy', in M. Beech and S. Lee (eds) *Ten Years of New Labour.* Basingstoke, Hampshire: Palgrave Macmillan.

Driver, S. and Martell, L. (1998) *New Labour – Politics after Thatcherism.* Cambridge: Polity Press.

Department of Trade and Industry (DTI) (1995) *Competitiveness: Forging Ahead.* London: HMSO.

— (1998) *Our Competitive Future: Building the Knowledge Driven Economy* (Cm. 4176). London: The Stationary Office.

Dyson, A., Farrell, P., Kerr, K. and Mearns, N. (2009) '"Swing, swing together": Multi-agency work in the new children's services', in C. Chapman and H. M. Gunter (eds) *Radical Reforms. Perspectives on an Era of Educational Change.* Abingdon, Oxen: Routledge (pp.155–68).

Earl, L. M., Watson, N., Levin, B., Leithwood, K., Fullan, M. and Torrance, N. (2003) *Watching and Learning 3: Final Report of the External Evaluation of England's National Literacy and Numeracy Strategies.* Nottingham: DfES Publications.

Edwards, T. and Whitty, G. (1992) 'Parental choice and educational reform in Britain and the United States', *British Journal of Educational Studies.* 40(2): 101–17.

Eggins, H. (ed.) (2003) *Globalisation and Reform in Higher Education.* Buckingham: Open University Press.

Eggleston, J. (1977) *The Sociology of the School Curriculum.* London: Routledge and Kegan Paul.

Ertl, H. and Wright, S. (2008) 'Reviewing the literature on the student learning experience in higher education', *London Review of Education.* 6(3), 195–210.

Exley, S. and Ball, S. J. (2011) 'Something old, something new: Understanding conservative education policy', in H. Bochel (ed.) *The Conservative Party and Social Policy.* Cambridge: Policy Press (pp.97–117).

Fairclough, N. (2000) *New Labour, New Language.* London: Routledge.

Faulks, K. (2006) 'Education for citizenship in England's secondary schools: A critique of current principles and practice', *Journal of Education Policy.* 21(1): 59–74.

Ferlie, E., Ashburner, L., Fitzgerald, L. and Pettigrew, A. (1996) *The New Public Management in Action.* Oxford: Oxford University Press.

Flude, M. and Hammer, M. (eds) (1990) *The Education Reform Act, 1988 – Its Origins and Implications.* London: Falmer Press.

Finegold, D. (1993) 'The emerging post-16 system: Analysis and critique', in W. Richardson, J. Woolhouse and D. Finegold (eds) *The Reform of Post 16 Education and Training in England and Wales.* Harlow: Longman.

Finegold, D., Keep, E., Miliband, D., Raffe, D., Spours, K. and Young, M. (1990) *A British Baccalaureate: Overcoming Division Between Education and Training.* London: Institute for Public Policy Research.

Flynn, N. (1999) 'Modernising British Government', *Parliamentary Affairs.* 52(4): 582–97.

Forrester, G. (2000) 'Professional autonomy versus managerial control: The experience of teachers in an English primary school', *International Studies in Sociology of Education.* 10(2): 133–51.

— (2005) 'All in a day's work: Primary teachers "performing" and "caring"', *Gender and Education.* 17(3): 271–87.

— (2011) 'Performance management in education: Milestone or millstone?' *Management in Education.* 25(1): 5–9.

Forrester, G. and Gunter, H. M. (2009) 'The academic work, identities and cultures of education leadership researchers in UK'. Paper presented to the American Educational Research Association (AERA) Annual Meeting, San Diego, USA, 13–17 April.

Foskett, N., Roberts, D. and Maringe, F. (2006) 'Changing fee regimes and their impact on student attitudes to higher education', *Report of a Higher Education Academy Funded Research Project 2005–2006.* Southampton: University of Southampton. Available at: http://hca.ltsn.ac.uk/assets/documents/research/changing_fees_regimes_full_report.pdf

Foucault, M. (1988) 'Sexuality, morality and the law', in *Michel Foucault: Politics, Philosophy, Culture. Interviews and Other Writings.* New York: Routledge.

— (1980) 'Truth and power', in C. Gordon (ed.) *Power/Knowledge: Selected Interviews and Other Writings 1972–1977.* Brighton: Harvester.

— (2002) *Michel Foucault – Power Volume 3 – the Essential Works of Foucault 1954–1984,* J. D. aubion (ed.). London: Penguin.

Freeden, M. (2003) *Ideology – a Very Short Introduction.* Oxford: Oxford University Press.

Freire, P. ([1970] 1993) *Pedagogy of the Oppressed* (revised edn). London: Penguin.

Fuller, A. and Heath, S. (2010). 'Educational decision-making, social networks and the new widening participation', in M. David (ed.), *Improving Learning by Widening Participation in Higher Education.* London: Routledge (pp. 132–46).

Further Education Unit (FEU) (1979) *A Basis for Skills.* London: FEU.

Galton, M., Simon, B. and Croll, P. (1980) *Inside the Primary Classroom.* London: Routledge and Kegan Paul.

Gallagher, A. (2009) David Cameron sets out his vision for 'big society', *The Guardian*. Tuesday 10 November. www.guardian.co.uk/politics/video/2009/nov/10/david-cameron-hugo-young-lecture?intcmp=239 [accessed 15 June 2011].

Gamble, A. (1988) *The Free Economy and the Strong State*. London: Macmillan.

— (2009) *The Spectre at the Feast – Capitalist Crisis and the Politics of Recession*. Basingstoke: Palgrave Macmillan.

Garratt, D. (2011) 'Reflections on learning: Widening capability and the student experience', *Cambridge Journal of Education*. 41(2): 211–25.

Garratt, D. and Hammersley-Fletcher, L. (2009) 'Academic identities in Flux: Ambivalent articulations in a post-1992 university', *Power and Education*. 1(3): http://dx.doi.org/10.2304/power.2009.1.3.307

Garratt, D. and Piper, H. (2008a) *Citizenship Education, Identity and Nationhood – Contradictions in Practice?* London: Continuum.

— (2008b) 'Citizenship education in England and Wales: Theoretical critique and practical considerations', *Teachers and Teaching: Theory and Practice*. 14(5–6): 481–96.

— (2010) 'Heterotopian cosmopolitan citizenship education?' *Education, Citizenship and Social Justice*. 5(2): 43–55.

— (2012 in press) 'Citizenship education and philosophical enquiry: Putting thinking back into practice', *Education, Citizenship and Social Justice*.

Gewirtz, S. (1998) 'Conceptualizing social justice: Mapping the territory', *Journal of Education Policy*. 13(4): 469–84.

— (2002) *The Managerial School. Post-welfarism and Social Justice in Education*. London: Routledge.

Gewirtz, S., Ball, S. and Bowe, R. (1994) 'Parents, Privilege and the Education Market-place', *Research Papers in Education*. 9(1): 3–29.

— (1995) *Markets, Choice and Equity in Education*. Buckingham: Open University Press.

Giddens, A. (1987) *Social Theory and Modern Sociology*. Cambridge: Polity.

— (1990) *The Consequences of Modernity*. Cambridge: Polity Press.

— (1994) *Beyond Left and Right: The Future of Radical Politics*. Cambridge: Polity Press.

— (1998) *The Third Way: The Renewal of Social Democracy*. Cambridge: Polity Press.

— (2000) *The Third Way and Its Critics*. Cambridge: Polity Press.

Gillborn, D. (1998) 'Racism, selection, poverty and parents: New Labour, old problems?' *Journal of Education Policy*. 13(6): 717–35.

— (2005) 'Education policy as an act of white supremacy: Whiteness, critical race theory and education reform', *Education Policy*. 20: 485–505.

— (2009) 'Education policy as an act of white supremacy', in E. Taylor, D. Gillborn and G. Ladson-Billings (eds) *Foundations of Critical Race Theory in Education*. London: Routledge (pp. 51–69).

Gillborn, D. and Youdell, D. (2000) *Rationing Education – Policy, Practice, Reform and Equity*. Buckingham: Open University Press.

Gilpin, R. (1992) *The Political Economy of International Relations*. Princeton, NJ: Princeton University Press.

— (1987) *There ain't no Black in the Union Jack*. London: Hutchinson.

— (2004) *After Empire: Melancholia or Convivial Culture*. Oxfordshire: Routledge.

Gove, M. (2009) Failing schools need new leadership. Speech, Wednesday 7 October. www. conservatives.com/News/Speeches/2009/10/Michael_Gove_Failing_schools_need_new_ leadership.aspx [accessed 20 June 2011].

Government White Paper (1994) *Competitiveness – Helping Business to Win*. London: HMSO.

Grace, G. (1987) 'Teachers and the state in Britain: A changing relation', in M. Lawn and G. Grace (eds) *Teachers: The Culture and Politics of Work*. Lewes: Falmer Press.

Green, A. (1990) *Education and State Formation: The Rise of Education Systems in England, France and the USA*. Basingstoke: Palgrave.

— (1997) 'Core skills, general education and unification in post-16 education', in A. Hodgson and K. Spours (eds) *Dearing and Beyond: 14–19 Qualifications, Frameworks and Systems*. London: Kogan Page.

Grek, S. (2009) 'Governing by numbers: The PISA "effect" in Europe', *Journal of Educational Policy*. 24(1): 23–37.

The Guardian (2011) 'Losing the argument', *The Guardian*. Tuesday 8 February, p. 34.

Gunter, H. M. (ed) (2010) *The State and Education Policy: The Academies Programme*. London: Continuum.

Gunter, H. M. and Forrester, G. (2008a) 'New labour and school leadership 1997–2007', *British Journal of Educational Studies*. 56(2): 144–62.

— (2008b) *Knowledge Production in Educational Leadership (KPEL) Project*. Final Report to the ESRC. RES-000-23–1192.

— (2009) 'Institutionalised governance: The case of the national college for school leadership', *International Journal of Public Administration*. 32: 349–69.

— (2010) 'New labour and the logic of practice in educational reform', *Critical Studies in Education*. 51(1): 55–69.

Halpin, D. and Troyna, B. (1995) 'The politics of education policy borrowing', *Comparative Education*. 31(3): 303–10.

Hall, D. and Raffo, C. (2009) 'New Labour and breaking the education and poverty link: A conceptual account of its educational policies', in C. Chapman and H. M. Gunter (eds) *Radical Reforms – Perspectives on an Era of Educational Change*. Abingdon, Oxen: Routledge (pp. 155–68).

Hand, M. and Pearce, J. (2009) 'Patriotism in British schools: Principles, practices and press hysteria', *Educational Philosophy and Theory*. 41(4): 453–65.

Hansard (1870) *Hansard's Parliamentary Debates (Third Series: Vol. CC. 16 March to 29 April 1870, Second Volume of the Session)*. London: Cornelius Buck.

Hari, J. (2010) 'Welcome to Cameron land', *The Independent*. Wednesday 5 May. www.independent.co.uk/opinion/commentators/johann-hari/johann-hari-welcome-to-cameron-land-1962318.html.

Harris, A. and Chapman, C. (2004) 'Towards differentiated improvement for schools in challenging circumstances', *British Journal of Educational Studies*. 52(4): 417–31.

Hartley, D. (2003) 'New Economy, New Pedagogy?' *Oxford Review of Education*. 29(1): 81–94.

Harvey, D. (1990) *The Condition of Postmodernity: An Enquiry into the Conditions of Cultural Change*. Oxford: Blackwell.

— (1993) 'Class relations, social justice and the politics of difference', in J. Squires (ed.) *Principled Positions: Postmodernism and the Rediscovery of Value*. London: Lawrence and Wishart (pp. 85–120).

— (2010) *The Enigma of Capital and the Crises of Capitalism*. Cambridge: Polity Press.

Held, D., McGrew, A., Goldblatt, D. and Perraton, J. (1999) *Global Transformations*. Cambridge: Polity Press.

Helle, L. and Klemelä, K. (2010) 'Like a rolling stone? Recent trends in Finnish upper secondary education', in D. S. Beckett (ed.), *Secondary Education in the 21st Century*. New York: Nova Science Publishers, Inc.

Henkel, M. (2000) *Academic Identities and Policy Change in Higher Education*. London: Jessica Kingsley.

Henry, M., Lingard, B., Rizvi, F. and Taylor, S. (2008) *The OECD, Globalisation and Education Policy*. Bingley, UK: Emerald Group Publishing Ltd.

Higher Education Funding Council for England (HEFCE) (2004) *Widening Participation and Fairer Access Research Strategy*. Bristol: HEFCE.

Hodgson, A. and Spours, K. (1997) 'From the 1991 white paper to the Dearing report: A conceptual and historical framework for the 1990s', in A. Hodgson and K. Spours, *Dearing and Beyond 14–19 Qualifications, Frameworks and Systems*. London: Kogan Page.

— (1999) *New Labour's Educational Agenda. Issues and Policies for Education and Training from 14±*. London: Kogan Page.

— (2002) 'Key skills for all? The key skills qualification and Curriculum 2000', *Journal of Education Policy*. 17(1): 29–47.

— (2006) 'An analytical framework for policy engagement: The contested case of 14–19 reform in England', *Journal of Education Policy*. 21(6): 679–96.

Hodkinson, P. and Sparkes, A. (1995) 'Markets and vouchers: The inadequacy of individualist policies for vocational education and training in England and Wales', *Journal of Education Policy*. 10(2): 189–207.

Hoffman, J. (2004) *Citizenship Beyond the State*. London: Sage.

Home Office (2001a) '*Community Cohesion': A Report of the Independent Review Team (Cantle Report)*. London: Home Office.

— (2001b) *The Report of the Ministerial Group on Public Order and Community Cohesion (Denham Report)*. London: Home Office.

— (2002) *Secure Borders, Safe Haven: Integration with Diversity in Modern Britain*. London: Home Office.

— (2005) *Life in the United Kingdom: A Journey to Citizenship*. London: TSO.

Hood, C. (1995) 'Contemporary public management: A new global paradigm?' *Public Policy and Administration*. 10(2): 104–17.

Hurst, P. (1981) 'Aid and Educational Development: Rhetoric and Reality', *Comparative Education.* 17(2): 117–25.

Illich, I. (1971) *Deschooling Society.* London: Calder and Boyers.

Illich, I. and Verne, E. (1976) *Imprisoned in the Global Classroom.* London: Writers and Readers Publishing Cooperative.

Jarvis, P. (2000) 'The changing university: Meeting a need and needing to change', *Higher Education Quarterly.* 54(1): 43–67.

Jessop, B. (2002) *The Future of the Capitalist State.* Cambridge: Polity Press.

Jerome, L. (2009) 'New Labour, new citizens: Citizenship education as the creation of "model" citizens', Paper presented at Liverpool John Moores University, in the 'Working with Young People and Children' Seminar Series, 24 April, in Liverpool.

Johnson, N. (1990) *Reconstructing the Welfare State. A Decade of Change 1980–1990.* London: Harvester Wheatsheaf.

Johnson, P. (2004) 'Education Policy in England', *Oxford Review of Economic Policy.* 20(2): 173–97.

Johnson, R. and Steinberg, D. (2004) 'Distinctiveness and difference within New Labour', in D. Steinberg and R. Johnson (eds) *Blairism and the War of Persuasion.* London: Lawrence & Wishart.

Jones, G. E. (1992) 'Education in Wales: A different 'Great Debate'?', in M. Williams, R. Daugherty and F. Banks (eds) *Continuing the Education Debate.* London: Cassell.

Jones, K. (1991) *The Making of Social Policy in Britain: 1830–1990.* London: The Athlone Press.

Jones, K. (2003) *Education in Britain: 1944 to the Present.* Cambridge: Polity Press.

Jones, N. (1999) *Sultans of Spin.* London: Victor Gollancz.

Jones, P. W. (1988) *International Policies for Third World Education: UNESCO, Literacy and Development.* London and New York: Routledge.

Jupp, V. (1996) 'Documents and critical research', in R. Sapsford and V. Jupp (eds) *Data Collection and Analysis.* London: Sage Publications Ltd.

Kellner, D. (2000) 'Globalisation and new social movements: Lessons for critical theory and pedagogy', in N. C. Burbules and C. A. Torres (eds) *Globalisation and Education: Critical Perspectives.* London: Routledge (pp. 299–321).

Kay-Shuttleworth, J. (1868) 'Memorandum on popular education', in A. Pollard (ed.) (1996) *Readings for Reflective Teaching in the Primary School.* London: Cassell.

Keay, D. (1987) 'Aids, education and the year 2000!' *Women's Own.* 31 October, pp. 8–10.

Keep, E. (2005) 'Reflections on the curious absence of employers, labour market incentives and labour market regulation in English 14–19 policy: First signs of a change in direction?', *Journal of Education Policy.* 20(5): 533–53.

Keep, E. and Mayhew, K. (2004) 'The economic and distributional implications of current policies on higher education', *Oxford Review of Economic Policy.* 20(2): 298–314.

Kemp, J. (2011) 'Competition for places at Scottish universities will be fierce in 2012', *The Guardian.* 12 September, www.guardian.co.uk/education/2011/sep/12/scottish-universities-uk-students-fees [accessed 23 September 2011].

King, D. S. (1987) *The New Right: Politics, Markets and Citizenship.* London: Macmillan.

Kiwan, D. (2008) *Education for Inclusive Citizenship.* London: Routledge.

Kymlicka, W. (1995) *Multicultural Citizenship.* Oxford: Oxford University Press.

— (2002) *Contemporary Political Philosophy.* Oxford: Oxford University Press.

Lauder, H., Brown, P., Dillabough, J. A. and Halsey, A. H. (eds) (2006) *Education, Globalization and Social Change.* Oxford: Oxford University Press.

Lawton, D. (1980) *The Politics of the School Curriculum.* London: Routledge and Kegan Paul.

Leaton Gray, S. (2006) *Teachers under Siege.* Stoke-on-Trent: Trentham Books.

Legge, K. (1995) *Human Resource Management – Rhetorics and Realities.* Basingstoke: Macmillan Business.

Le Grand, J. (1998) 'The third way begins with CORA', *New Statesman.* 6 March, 26–7.

Leitch, S. (2006) *Prosperity for All in the Global Economy – World Class Skills. Final Report of the Leitch Review of Skills.* London: HMSO/HM Treasury.

Leonard, P. (1997) *Postmodern Welfare: Reconstructing an Emancipatory Project.* London: Sage.

Levacic, R. (1995) *Local Management of Schools: Analysis and Practice.* Milton Keynes: Open University Press.

Levitas, R. (1998) *The Inclusive Society? Social Exclusion and New Labour.* Basingstoke: Palgrave.

Londinium (2008) 'MPs demand tighter immigration controls', *The London Echo – Politics News for London.* 22 October, www.londonecho.com/20081022363/mps-demand-tighter-immigration-controls.html [accessed 18 August 2009].

Lowe, R. (1993) *The Welfare State in Britain Since 1945.* Basingstoke: Macmillan.

McGrew, A. (1992) 'A Global Society?' in S. Hall, D. Held and T. McGrew (eds) *Modernity and Its Futures.* Cambridge: Polity Press (pp. 61–102).

Mahony, P., Hextall, I. and Menter, I. (2002) 'Threshold assessment: Another peculiarity of the English or more McDonaldisation?' *International Studies in Sociology of Education.* 12(2): 145–68.

Mason, D. (2000) *Race and Ethnicity in Modern Britain.* Oxford: Oxford University Press.

— (2006) 'Ethnicity', in G. Payne (ed.), *Social Divisions.* Basingstoke: Palgrave (pp. 102–30).

Maylor, U., Read, B., Mendick, H., Ross, A. and Rollock, N. (2007) *Diversity and Citizenship in the Curriculum: Research Review.* (Brief No RB819.). London: DfES.

Meikle, J. (2011) 'English Defence League filling vacuum left by mainstream parties, says report', *The Guardian.* 22 September, www.guardian.co.uk/world/2011/sep/22/far-right-doorstep-hearts-minds [accessed 23 September 2011].

Miles, R. (1993) *Racism after Race Relations.* London: Routledge.

Miliband, D. (2006) 'Choice and voice in personalised learning', in Centre for Educational Research and Innovation (ed.) *Personalised Education.* Paris, France: OECD. Available from: www.oecd.org/dataoecd/50/41/41175554.pdf [accessed 20 May 2011].

Miller, D. (1999) *Principles of Social Justice.* Cambridge, MA: CUP.

— (2000) *Citizenship and National Identity.* Cambridge: Polity Press.

Mirza, H. S. (2007) 'Understanding the multicultural malaise', *Multiverse – Exploring Diversity and Achievement*, www.multiverse.ac.uk/attachments/335aecf3-a096–438d-a121–608-e86a8d2a5.pdf [accessed 8 September 2009].

Ministry of Education (MoE) (1959) *15 to 18: Report of the Central Advisory Council for Education – England (Vol. 1)*. London: HMSO.

Modood, T. (2007) *Multiculturalism*. Cambridge: Polity.

Moore, R. (1984) 'Schooling and the World of Work', in I. Bates, J. Clarke, P. Cohen, D. Finn, R. Moore and P. Willis (eds) *Schooling for the Dole*. London: Macmillan.

Morley, L. (2003) *Quality and Power in Higher Education*. Maidenhead: Open University Press.

Moser Report (1999) *Improving Literacy and Numeracy: A Fresh Start*. London: DfES.

Mulholland, H. and Vesagar, J. (2011) 'Willetts forced on to back foot over premium rate university places', *The Guardian*. 10 May, www.guardian.co.uk/education/2011/may/10/plan-rich-pay-extra-university-places-entrench-privilege [accessed 15 May 2011].

Mullard, C. (1973) *Black Britain*. London: Allen and Unwin.

Mundy, K. (1998) 'Educational multilateralism and world (dis)order', *Comparative Education Review*. 42(4): 448–78.

Murray, R. (1989) 'Fordism and post-Fordism', in S. Hall and M. Jacques (eds) *New Times: The Changing Face of Politics in the 1990s*. London: Lawrence Wishart (pp. 38–53).

National Curriculum Council (NCC) (1990) *Curriculum Guidance 8 – Education for Citizenship*. York: NCC.

National College for School Leadership (NCSL) (2002) *Prime Minister Performs Official NCSL Opening*. NCSL press release, 25 October 2002.

Neill, A. S. (1968) *Summerhill*. Harmondsworth: Penguin Books.

Nozick, R. (1974) *Anarchy, State and Utopia*. Oxford: Wiley-Blackwell.

Nussbaum, M. (2000) *Women and Human Development: The Capabilities Approach*. Cambridge: Cambridge University Press.

O'Neill, M. (1995) 'Introduction', in D. S. G. Carter and M. H. O'Neill (eds) *International Perspectives on Educational Reform and Policy Implementation*. London: RoutledgeFalmer (pp. 1–10).

Office for Standards in Education, Children's Services and Skills (OfSTED) (2005) *Primary National Strategy. An Evaluation of its Impact in Primary Schools 2004/05*. Ref. HMI 2396. OfSTED.

Organisation for Economic Cooperation and Development (OECD) (2004) *Policy Brief: Lifelong Learning*. Paris: OECD.

Olssen, M. (2004) 'From the Crick Report to the Parekh report: Multiculturalism, cultural difference and democracy – the re-visioning of citizenship education', *British Journal of Sociology of Education*. 25(2): 179–92.

Osler, A. (2008) 'Citizenship education and Ajegbo report: Re-imagining a cosmopolitan nation', *London Review of Education*. 6(1): 11–25.

— (2009) 'Patriotism, multiculturalism and belonging: Political discourse and the teaching of history', *Educational Review*. 61(1): 85–100.

Osler, A. and Starkey, H. (2001) 'Citizenship, human rights and cultural diversity', in A. Osler (ed.), *Citizenship and Democracy in Schools: Diversity, Identity and Equality*. Stoke-on-Trent: Trentham (pp. 19–32).

— (2005) *Changing Citizenship – Democracy and Inclusion in Education*. Maidenhead, Berks: Open University Press.

Ozga, J. (1995) 'Deskilling a profession: Professionalism, deprofessionalism and the new managerialism', in H. Busher and R. Saran (eds) *Managing Teachers as Professionals in Schools*. London: Kogan Page.

— (2000) *Policy Research in Educational Settings – Contested Terrain*. Buckingham: Open University Press.

Pantazis, C. and S. Pemberton (2009) 'From the "old" to the "new" suspect community – examining the impacts of recent counter-terrorist legislation', *The British Journal of Criminology*. 49: 646–66.

Paton, G. (2011) 'Graduate gloom as 83 students apply for every vacancy', *The Telegraph*. 28 June, www.telegraph.co.uk/education/8602101/Graduate-gloom-as-83-students-apply-for-every-vacancy.html [accessed 28 June 2011].

Patterson, S. (1963) *Dark Strangers: A Study of West Indians in London*. Harmondsworth: Penguin.

Payne, J. (2002) 'A tale of two curriculums: Putting the English and Norwegian curriculum models to the test of the "high skills" vision', *Journal of Education and Work*. 15(2): 118–43.

Phillips, A. (1997) 'From inequality to difference: A severe case of displacement', *New Left Review*. 224, 143–53.

Phillips, D. (2011) *The German Example. English Interest in Educational Provision in Germany Since 1800*. London: Continuum.

Phillips, R. and Furlong, J. (2001) *Education, Reform and the State – Twenty-five years of Politics, Policy and Practice*. London: RoutledgeFalmer.

Piore, D. and Sabel, C. (1984) *The Second Industrial Divide*. New York: Basic Books.

Pollard, A., Broadfoot, P., Croll, P., Osborn, M. and Abbott, D. (1994) *Changing English Primary Schools? The impact of the Education Reform Act at Key Stage 1*. London: Cassell

Pollitt, C. (1993) *Managerialism and the Public Services: Cuts or Cultural Change in the 1990s?* (2nd edn). Oxford: Blackwell Business.

Pring, R. (1986) 'Privatisation of education', in R. Rogers (ed.). *Education and Social Class*. Lewes: Falmer Press.

— (1992) 'Liberal education and vocational preparation', in M. Williams, R. Daugherty and F. Banks (eds) *Continuing the Education Debate*. London: Cassell.

— (2004) *Philosophy of Education*. London: Continuum (pp. 54–64).

— (2005) 'Labour government policy 14–19', *Oxford Review of Education*. 31(1): 71–85.

Prison Reform Trust (2011) 'Build the big society behind bars', *Prison Reform Trust Online*. 16 May, www.prisonreformtrust.org.uk/PressPolicy/News/vw/1/ItemID/129 [accessed 27 May 2011].

Pykett, J. (2007) 'Making citizens governable? The Crick Report as governmental technology', *Journal of Education Policy.* 22(3): 301–19.

Qualification and Curriculum Authority (QCA) (1998) *Education for Citizenship and the Teaching of Democracy in Schools (Crick Report).* London: QCA.

— (1999) *Citizenship.* London: QCA.

Rex, J. and Moore, R. (1967) *Race Community and Conflict.* London: Oxford University Press.

Raffe, D., Howieson, C., Spours, K. and Young, M. (1998) 'The unification of post-compulsory education: Towards a conceptual framework', *British Journal of Educational Studies.* 46(2): 169–87.

Rafferty, F. and Barnard, N. (1998) 'Blair warns teachers not to resist reforms', *Times Educational Supplement.* 2 October: 8.

Ranson, S. (1993) 'Markets or democracy for education', *British Journal of Educational Studies.* 41(4): 333–52.

— (1994) *Towards a Learning Society.* London: Continuum.

Rawls, J. (1999) *A Theory of Justice* (2nd edn). Oxford: Oxford University Press.

Rentoul, J. (1990) 'Individualism', in R. Jowell, S. Witherspoon, and L. Brook (eds) *British Social Attitudes – The Seventh Report.* Aldershot: Gower.

Resnik, J. (2006) 'International organizations, the "education-economic growth" black box and the development of world education culture', *Comparative Education Review.* 50(2): 173–95.

Reynolds, D. (1986) *School Effectiveness.* London: Falmer Press.

Richards, C. (1999) *Primary Education – At a Hinge of History?* London: Falmer Press.

Ritzer, G. F. (2008) *The McDonaldization of Society 5* (5th edn). Thousand Oaks, California: Pine Forge Press.

Rizvi, F. (2000) 'International education and the production of global imagination', in N. C. Burbules and C. A. Torres (eds) *Globalisation and Education: Critical Perspectives.* London: Routledge (pp. 205–25).

— (2004) 'Debating globalization and education after September 11', *Comparative Education.* 40(2): 157–71.

— (2009) 'International perspectives on social justice and education', in W. Ayers, T. Quinn, and D. Stovall (eds) *Handbook of Social Justice in Education.* Abingdon, Oxon: Routledge (pp. 91–4).

Robertson, R. (1992) *Globalization: Social Theory and Global Culture.* London: Sage.

— (1995) 'Glocalization: Time-space and homogeneity-heterogeneity', in M. Featherstone, S. Lash, and R. Robertson (eds) *Global Modernities.* London: Sage (pp. 25–44).

— (2005) 'Re-imagining and re-scripting the future of education: Global knowledge economy discourses and the challenge to education systems', *Comparative Education.* 41(2): 151–70.

Rose, J. (2009) *Independent Review of the Primary Curriculum: Final Report.* Nottingham: DCSF Publications.

Rosenau, J. (ed.) (1992) *Governance without Government: Order and Change in World Politics.* Cambridge: Cambridge University Press.

Rosenau, J. and Singh, J. P. (eds) (2002) *Information Technologies and Global Politics: The Changing Scope of Power and Governance.* Albany, NY: State University of New York Press.

Rothenberg, L. (2003) 'The Three Tensions of Globalisation', *Issues in Global Education.* 175: 3–6.

Rowan, P. (1997) 'From one extreme to the other', *TES Magazine.* 25 April 1997, www.tes.co.uk/article.aspx?storycode=47075 [accessed 21 April 2011].

Rowley, E. (2010) 'UK's total debt forecast to hit £10 trillion by 2015', *The Telegraph.* 9 November 2010, www.telegraph.co.uk/finance/economics/8118467/UKs-total-debt-forecast-to-hit-10-trillion-by-2015.html [accessed 24 June 2011].

— (2011) 'Unemployment figures raise fears UK is in jobless recovery', *The Telegraph.* 17 February 2011, www.telegraph.co.uk/finance/economics/8329285/Unemployment-figures-raise-fears-UK-is-in-jobless-recovery.html [accessed 17 February 2011].

Scott, P. (2011) 'The white paper is a mess. It does not do what it says on the tin', *Education Guardian.* Tuesday 5 July, p.2.

Scruton, R. (1980) *The Meaning of Conservatism.* Harmondworth: Penguin.

Sedghi, A. and Shepherd, J. (2011) 'Tuition fees 2012: What are the universities charging?' *The Guardian.* 23 June 2011, www.guardian.co.uk/news/datablog/2011/mar/25/higher-education-universityfunding [accessed 23 September 2011].

Sen, A. (1992) *Inequality Re-examined.* Oxford: Oxford University Press.

— (1999) *Development as Freedom.* Oxford: Oxford University Press.

Shepherd, J. (2009) 'Tories pledge to make schools 'engines of social change', *The Guardian.* Friday 6 November, www.guardian.co.uk/politics/2009/nov/06/tories-michael-gove-education [accessed 1 June 2011]

— (2010) 'UK schools slip down world rankings', *The Guardian.* 7 December, www.guardian.co.uk/education/2010/dec/07/uk-schools-slip-world-rankings?INTCMP=SRCH [accessed 20 May 2011].

— (2011) 'Private university BPP launches bid to run 10 publicly funded counterparts', *The Guardian.* 21 June, www.guardian.co.uk/education/2011/jun/21/bpp-private-bid-run-public-universities [accessed 28 June 2011].

Silver, H. (1990) *Education, Change and the Policy Process.* London: The Falmer Press.

Simon, B. (1967) *Education and the Labour Movement 1870–1920.* London: Lawrence and Wishart.

— (1991) *Education and the Social Order – British Education since 1944.* London: Lawrence and Wishart.

Smithers, R. (2002) 'Government fails to meet targets for 11-year-olds', *The Guardian.* 27 September, www.guardian.co.uk/politics/2002/sep/27/uk.schools?INTCMP=SRCH [accessed 7 March 2011].

Sparrow, A. (2011) 'Cameron attacks 'state multiculturalism', *The Guardian.* 26 February, www.guardian.co.uk/politics/2008/feb/26/conservatives.race [accessed 3 March 2011].

Speaker's Commission on Citizenship (1990) *Encouraging Citizenship: Report of the Commission on Citizenship.* London: HMSO.

Spear, C. E. (1999) 'The changing pressures on primary schools', in C. Chitty and J. Dunford (eds) *State Schools – New Labour and the Conservative Legacy*. London: Woburn Press.

Spours, K. (1995) *Issues of Post-16 Participation, Attainment and Progression*, Working Paper No 17, Post-16. Education Centre, London: London University Institute of Education.

— (1997) 'GNVQs and the Future of Broad Vocational Qualifications', in A. Hodgson and K. Spours (eds) *Dearing and Beyond 14–19 Qualifications, Frameworks and Systems*. London: Kogan Page.

Steiner, R. ([1907] 1996) *The Education of the Child*. London: Steiner Books.

Stiglitz, J. (2002) *Globalization and its Discontents*. London: Penguin Books.

Straw, J. (2007) 'We need a British story – nationality should not require individuals to give up distinctive cultural attributes', *The Sunday Times*. 29 April, www.timesonline.co.uk/tol/comment/columnists/guest_contributors/article1720 [accessed 23 July 2009].

Stronach, I. (1988) 'Vocationalism and economic recovery: The case against witchcraft', in S. Brown and R. Wake (eds) *Education in Transition*. Edinburgh: Scottish Council for Research in Education.

Sullivan, M. (1992) *The Politics of Social Policy*. Hemel Hempstead: Harvester Wheatsheaf.

— (1994) *Modern Social Policy. Hemel Hempstead*: Harvester Wheatsheaf.

Tan, J. and Gopinathan, S. (2000) 'Education reform in Singapore: Towards greater creativity and innovation?' *NIRA Review*. 7(3): 5–10.

Taylor, C. (1992) *Multiculturalism and 'The Politics of Recognition'*. Princeton: Princeton University Press.

Taylor, E. (2009) 'The foundations of critical race theory in education: An introduction', in E. Taylor, D. Gillborn and G. Ladson-Billings (eds) *Foundations of Critical Race Theory in Education*. London: Routledge (pp. 1–13).

Teacher Training Agency (TTA) (1997) *Standards for the Award of Qualified Teacher Status*. London: Teacher Training Agency.

— (1998a) *National Standards for SENCOs, Subject Leaders and Headteacher*. London: Teacher Training Agency.

— (1998b) *National Standards for Headteachers*. London: Teacher Training Agency.

The Telegraph (2011) 'David Cameron says reform of education is the only way to tackle record youth unemployment', *The Telegraph*. 14 April 2011, www.telegraph.co.uk/finance/economics/8447318/David-Cameron-says-reform-of-education-is-the-only-way-to-tackle-record-youth-unemployment.html [accessed 14 April 2011].

Thrupp, M. and Tomlinson, S. (2005) 'Introduction: Education policy, social justice and "complex hope"', *British Educational Research Journal*. 31(5): 549–56.

Toffler, A. (1990) *Powershift*. New York: Bantam.

Tomlinson, J. (1993) *The Control of Education*. London: Cassell.

Tomlinson, S. (2001) *Education in a Post-welfare Society*. Buckingham: Open University Press.

— (2008a) *Race and Education – Policy and Politics in Britain*. Maidenhead: Open University Press.

— (2008b) *Education in a Post-welfare Society* (2nd edn). Maidenhead: Open University Press.

Trowler, P. (2003) *Education Policy* (2nd edn). London: Routledge

Troyna, B. (1993) *Racism and Education*. Buckingham: Open University Press.

The Stationery Office (TSO) (2002) *Nationality, Immigration and Asylum Act 2002*. London: TSO.

Vasagar, J. (2011) 'Tuition fees will mean fewer university entrants, warns LSE study', *The Guardian*. 7 September, www.guardian.co.uk/education/2011/sep/07/tuition-fees-rise-fewer-university-entrants-lse [accessed 23 September 2011].

Vasagar, J. and Shepherd, J. (2011) 'UK tuition fees are third highest in developed world, says OECD', *The Guardian*. 13 September, www.guardian.co.uk/education/2011/sep/13/uk-young-people-education-oecd [accessed 23 September 2011].

Walford, G. (2000) 'From City Technology Colleges to Sponsored Grant-maintained Schools', *Oxford Review of Education*. 26(2): 145–58.

Walker, E. (2008) 'Are degrees worth the paper they're printed on?' *The Independent Higher*. 8 September, www.independent.co.uk/news/education/higher/are-degrees-worth-the-paper-theyre-printed-on-922410.html [accessed 15 April 2011].

Walker, M. (2008) 'Widening participation; widening capability', *London Review of Education*. 6, 267–79.

Walker, M. and Unterhalter, E. (2007) 'The capability approach: It's potential for work in education', in M. Walker and E. Unterhalter (eds) *Amartya Sen's Capability Approach and Social Justice in Education*. Basingstoke, Hampshire: Palgrave Macmillan (pp. 1–8).

Wallerstein, I. (2011) *Historical Capitalism with Capitalist Civilisation* (3rd edn). London: Verso.

Watkins, K. and Fowler, P. (2003) *Rigged Rules and Double Standards*. Oxford: Oxfam.

Watson, C. W. (2000) *Multiculturalism*. Buckingham: Open University Press.

Webb, R. (1993) 'The National Curriculum and the changing nature of topic work', *The Curriculum Journal*. 4(2): 239–51.

Webb, R. and Vulliamy, G. (1996) 'A deluge of directives: Conflict between collegiality and managerialism in the post-ERA primary school', *British Educational Research Journal*. 22(4): 441–58.

Webster, P. and O'Leary, J. (1999) 'Teacher "excuse culture" attacked by Blair', *The Times*. 21 October: 1.

West, A. (2006) 'School choice, equity and social justice: The case for more control', *British Journal of Educational Studies*. 54(1): 15–33.

White, J. (1982) *The Aims of Education Restated*. London: Routledge.

Whitty, G. (1990) 'The New Right and the National Curriculum', in M. Flude and M. Hammer (eds) *The Education Reform Act, 1988: Its Origins and Implications*. London: The Falmer Press.

— (2001) 'Education, social class and exclusion', *Journal of Education Policy*. 16(4): 287–95.

Wigborg, S. (2010) 'Learning Lessons from the Swedish Model', *FORUM*. 52(3): 279–84.

Wilkinson, J. R. (1999) 'Pre-school education in UK', in D. Matheson and I. Grosvenor (eds) *An Introduction to the Study of Education*. London: David Fulton Publishers (pp. 42–58).

Williams, F. (1989) *Social Policy: A Critical Introduction*. Cambridge: Polity Press.

Williams, L. (2009) 'Globalisation of education policy: Its effects on developing countries', in J. Zajda and V. Rust (eds) *Globalisation, Policy and Comparative Research – Discourses of Globalisation*. London: Springer (pp. 77–92).

Williams, M., Daugherty, R. and Banks, F. (eds) (1992) *Continuing the Education Debate*. London: Cassell.

Willms, J. D. and Echols, F. H. (1992) 'Alert and inert clients: The Scottish experience of parental choice of schools', *Economics of Education Review*. 11(4): 339–50.

Wohlstetter, P. and Anderson, L. (1994) 'What can US charter schools learn from England's grant-maintained schools?' *Phi Delta Kappan*. 75(February): 486–91.

Wolf, A. (2002) *Does Education Matter? Myths about Education and Economic Growth*. London: Penguin.

— (2004) 'Education and economic performance: Simplistic theories and their policy consequences', *Oxford Review of Economic Policy*. 20(2): 315–33.

— (2007) 'Round and round the houses: The Leitch review of skills', *Local Economic*. 22(2): 111–17.

— (2011) *Review of Vocational Education – The Wolf Report*. London: DFE.

Wolf, A., Jenkins, A. and Vignoles, A. (2006) 'Certifying the workforce: Economic imperative or failed social policy?' *Journal of Education Policy*. 21(5): 535–65.

Wolff, J. (2008) 'Social justice and public policy: A view from political philosophy', in G. Craig, D. Gordon and T. Burchardt (eds) *Social Justice and Public Policy: Seeking Fairness in Diverse Societies*. Bristol: Policy Press. (pp 17–32).

Woodhead, C. (2002) *Class War: The State of British Education*. London: Little, Brown & Company.

Woodward, W. (2007) 'Britain slumps in world league table for maths and reading', *The Guardian*. 5 December 2007, www.guardian.co.uk/uk/2007/dec/05/politics.schools?INTCMP=SRCH [accessed 20 May 2011].

Working Group on 14–19 Reform (2004) *14–19 Curriculum and Qualifications Reform: Final Report of the Working Group*. London: DfES.

Wyse, D., McCreery, E. and Torrance, H. (2008) *The Trajectory and Impact of National Reform: Curriculum and Assessment in English Primary Schools* (Primary Review Research Survey 3/2). Cambridge: University of Cambridge Faculty of Education.

Yeatman, A. (1994) *Postmodern Revisionings of the Political*. New York: Routledge.

Yosso, T. (2005) 'Whose culture has capital? A critical race theory discussion of community cultural wealth', *Race, Ethnicity and Education*. 8(1): 69–91.

Young, I. M. (1990) *Justice and the Politics of Difference*, Princeton. NJ: Princeton University Press.

— (2004) 'The ideal of community and the politics of difference', in C. Farrelly (ed.), *Contemporary Political Theory*. London: Sage (pp. 195–204).

Young, M. (1993) 'A curriculum for the 21st century? Towards a new basis for overcoming academic/vocational divisions', *British Journal of Educational Studies*. XXXXI(3): 203–22.

— (1997) 'The Dearing review of 16–19 qualifications: A step towards a unified system?' in A. Hodgson and K. Spours (eds) *Dearing and Beyond: 14–19 Qualifications, Frameworks and Systems*. London: Kogan Page (pp.25–39).

Young, M. and Leney, T. (1997) 'From A-levels to an advanced level curriculum of the future', in A. Hodgson and K. Spours (eds) *Dearing and Beyond 14–19 Qualifications, Frameworks and Systems*. London: Kogan Page (pp.40–56).

Zifcak, S. (1994) *New Managerialism: Administrative Reforms in Whitehall and Canberra*. Buckingham: Open University Press.

Index